AF538640

HUMAN RESOURCE DEVELOPMENT

AN INTEGRATED MODEL WITH
ORGANIZATIONAL CITIZENSHIP BEHAVIOUR

HUMAN RESOURCE DEVELOPMENT

AN INTEGRATED MODEL WITH ORGANIZATIONAL CITIZENSHIP BEHAVIOUR

By

Dr. Sheelam Jain

Faculty of HRMOB
Vignana Jyothi Institute of Management
Hyderabad

DISCOVERY PUBLISHING HOUSE
INDIA

Published by:

DISCOVERY PUBLISHING HOUSE
4383/4B, Ansari Road, Darya Ganj
New Delhi-110 002 (India)
Phone : +91-11-23279245; 23253475; 43596065
E-mail : discoverybooksindia@gmail.com
discoverypublishinghouse@gmail.com
namitwasan9@gmail.com
web : www.discoverypublishinggroup.com

First Edition: **2023**

ISBN: 978-81-958210-0-6

Human Resource Development:
An Integrated Model with Organizational Citizenship Behaviour

Printed at:
Infinity Imaging Systems
Delhi

Dedicated to my father, Shri Abhay Prakash Kothari and to my research mentor, Shri Ravindra Jain whose memories are unforgettable and support throughout is priceless.

Dedicated to the goal of contributing to research and development in the field of OB and HR.

Preface

Human Resource Development has been given much attention due to the sheer realization that human resources are the most valuable assets and their development and wellbeing is necessary to achieve competitive advantage in the contemporary world of work discerned by faster globalization, digitalization and technological advancements. It is also evident that the employee attitudes and behaviours still remain very important factors to examine in organizations because of their inherent nature to influence the overall efficiency and profitability of organizations. The integration of various HRD practices implemented by the organizations helps to create an environment which is conducive for the development of employee competencies and their wellbeing and in exchange employees are willing to 'go to that extra mile' and make significant and visible contribution to the organization's performance. Therefore, in this globally competitive and volatile external environment it has become imperative for HR professionals to foster development oriented workplace practices that focus on employee wellbeing, health and meaningful work and build a climate that fuels citizenship behaviours at workplaces. The book addresses the development focused bundles of HRD practices like performance appraisal, employee training, employee empowerment, organizational justice and work-life balance alongwith general HRD climate in an integrated form. This book also took a broader look into the HRD sub-systems category in an effort to discover new and meaningful relationships that HRD sub-systems share with organizational citizenship behaviour. Besides, the text also makes an attempt to study the aforementioned HRD sub-systems and organizational citizenship behaviours in public sector, private sector and foreign banks in India. As a result, recommendations are presented on how organizations design or remodel their HRD practices in ways that not only facilitates employee development but are also influential in promoting OCBs.

The book has been organized into three parts and eleven chapters. The first part, titled 'Introduction to Human Resource Development' comprises eight chapters and deals with the basics and fundamentals of HRD and its subsystems. The second part, 'Introduction to Organizational Citizenship

Behaviour' contains one chapter focuses on the basics and fundamentals of OCB and its dimensions. The third and last part, `Relationship between HRD and OCB', consists of two chapters, examining the relationship between HRD subsystems and OCB and presenting the results of measurement and assessment of the same in Indian Banking sector.

In the aforementioned endeavor, exhibits, figures and references have been provided to make the reading more illustrative, factual and meaningful. The book is intended to be useful for students, academicians, professionals and researchers to gain conceptual clarity and information on various topics and to understand the significance of developmental interventions supported by pragmatic research and possible recommendations. The author looks forward to receiving suggestions and feedback, from all the stakeholders at dr.sheelamjain@vjim.edu.in.

–Author

Contents

List of Abbreviations

DJ	Distributive Justice
EE	Employee Empowerment
ET	Employee Training
HRD	Human Resource Development
IJ	Interactional Justice
OCB	Organizational Citizenship Behaviour
OJ	Organizational Justice
PAS	Performance Appraisal System
PDM	Participative Decision Making
PJ	Procedural Justice
QWL	Quality of Work Life
SE	Self-Efficacy
WLB	Work-Life Balance

CHAPTER 1

Fundamentals of Human Resource Development

Introduction

The foundation of Human Resource Development (HRD) has been the belief that organizational, group or individual development is mediated through human expertise and effort. Development of Human Resources means growth through acquisition of capabilities that are needed not only to do the present job but also to perform well in the future expected job role. The most valuable assets of any organization, i.e., Human resources have unlimited potential capabilities that can be used only by creating an environment that can identify, develop and retain such capabilities. Human Resource Development (HRD) in organizations aims at creating such an environment to develop employee's capabilities and competencies. HRD systems are claimed to be vital components of overall HRM systems (Werner & DeSimone, 2006) because of their role in transferring competencies and capabilities around the overall organizational network.

Definition of HRD

The concept of HRD was initiated in 1969 by Dr. Leonard Nadler, who defined it as a set of systematic and planned activities designed by an organization to provide its members with the opportunities to learn necessary skills to meet current and future job demands and to produce behavioural changes. Rao (1986) elaborately defined HRD as a process by which employees of an organization are helped in a continuous and planned way to: (i) acquire or sharpen capabilities required to perform various functions associated with their present and future expected roles; (ii) develop their general capabilities as individuals and discover their own inner potential for own and/or organization development purposes; (iii) develop an organizational culture in which superior-subordinate relationships, teamwork and collaboration among sub-units are strong and contribute to the professional well-being, motivation and pride of employees. Thus, HRD is "a process for developing and unleashing human expertise through organization development and personnel training and development for the purpose of improving performance" (Swanson & Holton III, 2001). McLean and McLean (2001) identified the evolutionary nature of HRD and described it as "any process or activity that, either initially or over the long term, has the potential to develop work-based knowledge, expertise, productivity and satisfaction, whether for personal or group/team gain, or for the benefit of an organization, community, nation, or, ultimately, the whole of humanity". Rao, Abraham and Nair (1993) opined that the scope of HRD is two-fold: at one side, to developing competencies of human resource by enhancing knowledge, building skill, changing attitude and teaching values; and at other side, creation of conditions through public policy, programs and other interventions to help people to apply these competencies for their own and others' benefits and making things happen.

Purpose of HRD

The goal of HRD is to develop, the capabilities of each employee as an individual; the capabilities of each individual in relation to his or her present role as well as future expected role; the dyadic relationship between each employee and his or her supervisor; the team spirit and functioning in every organization/department/group; collaboration among different units of the organization; and, the organization's overall health and self-renewing capabilities, which, in turn, increase the enabling capabilities of individuals, dyads, teams, and the entire organization (Rao, 1986). In order to achieve these objectives, various HRD sub-systems such as employee training, performance appraisal and development, potential appraisal and development, feedback and counseling,career planning and development, job enrichment, employee empowerment, compensation and rewards management, employee welfare and quality of work life, etc. are to be well designed and implemented effectively. All these HRD sub-systems are designed to work together in an integrated system. In addition, top management's commitment to the investment of all sorts of human resources development is crucial. The values of openness, trust, mutuality, teamwork, collaboration and enthusiasm within the system should be recognized by every member of the organization. Such an integrated system when implemented properly through various interventions can contribute significantly to positive individual and organizational changes ultimately leading to improved individual and organizational performance.

HRD Subsystems

Different sets of HR practices have been proposed in the various research models and frameworks to influence organizational and individual development. Rao (1986) in his integrated HR systems suggested nine HRD process mechanisms or subsystems to achieve HRD goals. These sub-systems or practices were performance appraisal, potential appraisal and development, feedback and performance coaching, career planning, training, organizational development, rewards, HRIS, employee welfare and quality of work life. High-performance work system suggested by Appelbaum, Bailey, Berg, & Kalleberg (2000) identified five distinct HR practices viz., empowerment, competence development, information sharing, recognition and fair organizational rewards that may influence employee's work related attitudes and performance behaviours. Bamburger and Meshoulam (2000) proposed that an integrated measure of human resource or high-performance human resource practices should assess selective staffing, extensive skills training, broad career paths, promotion from within, guaranteed job security, results-oriented appraisal, extensive and open-ended rewards, broad job description, flexible job assignment, and encouragement of participation. Kandula (2001) in his strategic HRD framework proposed ten strategic HRD practices that directly affect the development of human resources. The proposed practices were training, performance appraisal, job enrichment, career planning, communication, involvement, empowerment, compensation, working conditions, family welfare and HRD department/ function. According to Swanson and Holton model the two primary components of HRD are organizational development and training and development and these two have connections with various applications and work contexts such as intellectual and social capital, workforce development, human resource management, organizational effectiveness, leadership and strategy, work system design, change management, process improvement, career development and quality improvement (Swanson & Holton, 2009). Jain, Premkumar and Kamble (2014) in their conceptual framework of HRD systems emphasized the functioning of HRD department, employee training, performance appraisal, job enrichment, career planning, employee communication, and employee empowerment as key sub-systems of HRD that positively impact productivity and adaptability of human resources. A careful analysis of the above mentioned models indicate that the choice of HRD dimensions in various conceptualizations and research models vary with few commonalities. Among all these models, Kandula's strategic HRD framework dealt with an exhaustive coverage of HRD sub-systems that directly affect the employee development. Practices such as training, performance appraisal and empowerment are frequently addressed in most HRD models, possibly due to their direct influence on employee attitudes and behaviours. However, we believe that HRD dimensions viz., quality of work life, career development and management development also significantly contribute to human resource development via direct or indirect effects on employee attitudes and behaviours. Of course all these dimensions of HRD contribute to their maximum capacity in presence of a supportive developmental climate, which is a pre-requisite for successful implementation of HRD practices.

1. **HRD Climate:** Human resource development aims at providing opportunities to individuals for full utilization and expansion of their potential and focuses on the creation of values and culture conducive to individual growth in the organizational context. Proponents claimed that the success of HRD in an organization depends to a large extent, on the existence of a favourable HRD climate. The objective of HRD in organizations is to create such a climate that is favourable to develop employee's capabilities and competencies. HRD climate is an integral part of organizational climate. Thus, the policies, procedures, culture and structure, all together, decides the extent to which employees are satisfied in an organization and ultimately influences their development, attitudes, behaviours and overall performance. Accordingly, it can be said that HRD climate of an organization can be assessed by measuring the perceptions of its employees about the developmental climate prevailing in the organization. An optimal level of developmental climate is essential for facilitating HRD activities and an organization that has better HRD climate and processes is likely to be more effective than an organization that does not have them (Rao, 1992). Most researchers agree that a congenial HRD climate is extremely important in order to achieve the HRD goals. The HRD climate can be characterized by tendencies such as treating employees as the most important resources, perceiving that developing employees is the job of every manager, believing in the capability of employees, communicating openly, encouraging risk taking and experimentation, making efforts to help employees recognize their strengths and weaknesses, creating a general climate of trust, collaboration and autonomy, supportive personnel policies, and supportive HRD practices (Rao & Abraham, 1986). When a significant number of employees in an organization internalize these values, there emerges a climate conducive for sustainable human resource development. The general climate is a combination of support from all the concerned quarters' viz., from the management people working at different levels, good supportive personnel policies and practices as well as the positive attitudes towards the development of the people vis-a-vis their organization (Schneider & Reichers, 1983; Chandra & Coeho, 1993). The HRD climate of an organization plays an important role in ensuring the competency, motivation and development of its employees (Patel, 2005). Clearly, it is the supportive climate that is essential for proper implementation of HRD practices.

2. **Performance Appraisal:** Performance appraisal is a formal, regular and systematic process of identifying, evaluating and developing the job performance of an employee in order to effectively achieve organizational goals. Thus, the ultimate objective of performance appraisal is to align individual goals and performance with the organizational goals and performance. The performance appraisal process benefits employees in terms of their performance improvement, recognition, feedback and offering career growth. Performance appraisals are considered to be the most essential element in creating positive work environment and involve a range of attributes, such as reward, communication, feedback, employee reactions, equity and fairness, trust and acceptance, attitudes towards conflict, and social context (Brown & Heywood, 2005; Erdogan, Kraimer & Liden., 2001; Lawler, 2003; Levy & Williams, 2004). Performance appraisal process has broadly two main purposes: first, to make administrative decisions (whether to terminate/retain/promote/increments, etc.) and second, to improve employee performance (by identifying the training needs and key result areas as well as improvement areas and help the employee to improve in those areas. Whether performance appraisals have held either administrative or developmental purposes, the ultimate goal of performance appraisal should be to provide information that will best enable managers to improve employee performance (DeNisi & Pritchard, 2006) and culminate directly to individual development and organizational development. It is a tool to encourage strong performers to maintain their high level of performance and to motivate poor performers to do better (Scott, 1980). Therefore, appraisals must be viewed as a mechanism for motivating as well as developing people and that is why, today, the focus of both practice and research has been moving towards developmental performance appraisal (Levy & Williams, 2004). A development oriented performance appraisal process includes setting up performance goals and standards, track employee's progress against the set goals, review actual performance, provide constructive and developmental feedback, rewards and recognition for superior performance, identifying training needs, and lastly agreeing on future performance and goals. Thus, the effectiveness of performance appraisal system is based on the extent to which the system is HRD oriented. An HRD oriented system promotes participative planning of performance, analysis of performance leading to the identification of factors facilitating and hindering performance, performance review discussions, relatively greater objective assessment through task and target orientation, identification of developmental needs, improved communication, openness and mutuality, and trust among appraisers and appraisees

(Rao, 1992). The importance of effective performance appraisal in organizations is thus underscored by the general notion that appraisals help to develop individuals, improve organizational performance and thus feed into business planning.

3. **Employee Training:** Employee training believed to be a traditional HRD practice, is defined as a learning process that involves the acquisition of knowledge, sharpening of skills, concepts, rules, or changing of attitudes and behaviours to enable the employees to perform job-related duties, accomplish specific tasks and meet the quality requirements of human resources for the future. Employee training is regarded as one of the most widespread human resources (HR) practices (Boselie, Dietz & Boon, 2005) and development of high potential workers with the support of the continuous training and retraining is seen as a core element in the development of competitive advantage of the organizations (Kandula, 2001). According to systematic approach to training, there are five phases of training process viz., (i) Analysis phase: which includes training needs analysis, training-needs assessment, performance analysis, job/task analysis, learner's analysis, content analysis, skill-gap analysis; (ii) Design phase: which includes stating training objectives, designing training deliverables, budgeting of training project, training scheduling, managing training project, and designing blue-prints and prototypes for training; (iii) Development phase: which includes drafting and creating reading materials, audio-visual aids, videos, softwares and also tests and feedback instruments; (iv) Implementation phase: which included classroom and non-classroom delivery of training and training of trainers; and (v) Evaluation phase: which includes evaluating trainees' reaction, evaluating learning, evaluating transfer of training and evaluating the results of training (Jain & Agrawal, 2007). The significance of employee training is two- fold: from the employee perspective, training helps them to perform their jobs effectively (Moskowitz, 2008) by making them suitable (Miller, 2002), eligible, skillful (Houlton, 1998), and a valuable resource (Prokopenko, 1987); from the organizational perspective, training programmes are expected to provide numerous benefits to the organization including employee development, increased productivity and improved employee performance (Gultek, Dodd & Guydosh, 2006; Watson, 2008). Thus, assessing training effectiveness can turn training into a powerful force for improvement of the business for both the organization and the people in it.

4. **Career Planning & Development:** Career development is an ongoing process of planning and directed action toward personal work and life goals. It is the outcome of the individual's career planning and

the organization's provision of support and opportunities, ideally a collaborative process (Simonsen, 1997). Career development is defined as a process of professional growth brought about by work-related learning, where the process apparently could be individually or organizationally driven (Van der Sluis & Poell, 2003). While career planning is the process of setting up career goals and deciding on action plans to achieve those goals, career development is related to individual improvements to achieve individual career goals. Career planning and development is thus, future-focused professional growth. Career development can be both formal and informal and may take place within and outside of the organization (Mc Donald & Hite, 2005). From the organizational perspective, career planning and development is concerned with upgradation of human resources to improve their productivity levels and it has gained a lot of importance with the increase in organizational size and complexity, advancements in technology and individual needs and aspirations. Traditionally, organizations have expected career development efforts to improve performance, increase retention, create a loyal and committed workforce, and support an effective succession plan (Gilley, Eggland & Gilley, 2002). Career planning provides employees with an opportunity to develop their careers and to strive toward specific job objectives. The success of organizational career planning and development initiatives requires strong commitment at every level with the supporting tools and processes to sustain it and hold managers accountable for how well they develop their subordinates. According to Gatewood and Rockmore (1986) career development can be achieved through two techniques: self-assessment, whereby employees are able to evaluate their fitness for specific jobs and, self-nomination, where employees are made aware of position openings as they occur and may express their interest for candidate consideration or by requesting for participation in training programs organized for employee development. According to Wils, Guerin and Bernard (1993), there are three types of career development activities conducted in organizations: (i) Impersonal career, focusing on three internal staffing activities: job posting, promotion-from-within and lateral mobility, (ii) Organizational career, consisting of five organization-oriented activities: succession planning, high potential management, data collection on employees, job matching and data collection on future jobs, and (iii) Individual career, including two individual-oriented activities: career planning and career counselling. Baruch (2004) proposed a six-dimension model of organizational career systems, which includes involvement, sophistication and complexity, strategic orientation, developmental focus, organizational decision-making focus, and innovation. Kim (2005) proposed two - dimensional taxonomy for career development interventions by the organization: (i) Individual-focused activities partially or entirely allow individuals to make decisions about their participation and includes training and development, career development support system and compensation/ benefit system and, (ii) Organizational-focused activities are operated primarily for organizational purposes, rather than individual benefit and it includes personnel allocation system and employee appraisal systems. Although the HRD literature has routinely discussed "management development" as separate from "career development", much of what traditionally has been described as "career development" has targeted managerial-level employees and excluded those in non-management tracks (McDonald, Hite, & Gilbreath, 2002). Both career and management development ensures the availability of efficient and satisfied employees with required skills, knowledge and talent. The literature supports that employees and systems can mutually benefit from the career development process, reinforcing its relevance as a human resource development function (van Dijk, 2004).

5. **Employee Empowerment:** Employee empowerment is considered to be one of the most powerful and effective HR practices that facilitates to make greatest contribution by the people who are capable of creating added value in product and service which is rare and inimitable (Ghosh, 2013). It is a process of orienting and enabling individuals to think, behave and take action in an autonomous way. Empowerment allows employees to assume different roles and responsibilities in the organizations and thus exert a greater influence at work while enjoying increased autonomy. Moreover, when employees experience empowerment and see the impact their jobs are having on the organization they identify more with the goals of the organization and as a result are more committed to it (Elloy, 2012). There are two approaches to employee empowerment: (a) Structural or relational empowerment, that focuses on management practices such as participation and involvement, autonomy, delegation of authority and information sharing, and (b) Psychological or motivational empowerment that emphasizes on an employee's psychological strengths and perceptions of power, competence, control and self-efficacy. Thus, structural empowerment focuses on the factors of the situation in which people work, whereas psychological empowerment focuses on a subjective assessment of how people feel as they perform their work. Other factors that facilitate empowerment at workplaces include informal organizational structure; flexible, participative and learning culture; reward and recognition system; non-routine and challenging jobs; access to resources and funds; degree of autonomy and selection of leader; leader as a role model; mutual trust; decision-

making; professional growth; status, and impact. Whilst earlier research focussed on empowerment as a set of management practices to delegate authority (discretionary empowerment) (Blau & Alba, 1982), recent research has centered on psychological empowerment, focusing on employee experience (Raub & Robert, 2013; Bhatnagar, 2005). However, few researchers (e.g., Cho & Faerman, 2010) have proposed an integrated model of empowerment addressing both structural as well as psychological empowerment, suggesting that structural empowerment leads to an increase in an individual's psychological empowerment. Kanter (1993) suggested that work environments that provide access to information, resources, support and the opportunity to learn and develop are empowering and enable employees to accomplish their work. Empowerment has been shown to predict important organizational outcomes, such as trust in management, organizational commitment, job satisfaction, lower levels of job stress, job involvement and career satisfaction (Noorliza & Hasni, 2006). The factors encompassing psychological or structural empowerment have a strong effect on employee development.

6. **Quality of Work Life:** Quality of work life has been defined as the workplace strategies, operations and environment that promote and maintain employee satisfaction with an aim to improving working conditions for employees and organizational effectiveness for employers. It is a measure of the quality of human experience which is a matter of the individual – organization interface (Guest, 1979). Certain working conditions and management practices such as, reasonable pay, healthy physical environment, employees' welfare, job security, equal treatment in job related matters, grievance handling, opportunity to grow and develop, good human relations, participation in decision making and balance in life are some of the key components of this humanistic and life-enhancing 'work environment'. Walton (1975) proposed eight major conceptual categories relating to QWL as, (1) adequate and fair compensation, (2) safe and healthy working conditions, (3) immediate opportunity to use and develop human capacities, (4) opportunity for continued growth and security, (5) social integration in the work organization, (6) constitutionalism in the work organization, (7) work and total life space and (8) social relevance of work life. Similarly, other researchers have suggested different factors of QWL and whilst some authors have emphasized the workplace aspects in QWL, others have identified the relevance of personality factors, psychological wellbeing, and broader concepts of happiness and life satisfaction. Besides improving the work system, QWL programmes usually emphasize development of employee skills, the reduction of occupational stress and the development of more co-

operative employment relations. In order to ensure better quality of work life, it is very important that the principles of justice, fair and equity should be taken care of in disciplinary procedure, grievance procedures, promotions, transfers, demotion, work assignment, leave, etc. Moreover, in the process of securing an economic prospect in the inflated financial scenario and due to increasing work place demands, personal and family responsibility is neglected thereby deteriorating the interaction of family life that reduces QWL. Thus, considering the significance of organizational justice and work-life balance in ensuring better quality of work life, it is intended to emphasize on these two components of QWL in the present study.

(a) **Organizational Justice:** Organizational justice (OJ) refers to the extent to which employee perceives workplace procedures, outcomes and interactions to be fair in nature. The dimensions of OJ are commonly conceptualized as distributive justice i.e., the fairness of decision outcomes, procedural justice i.e., the fairness of procedures leading to a particular outcome, and interactional justice which refers to the quality of interpersonal treatment received by employees particularly as part of formal decision making procedures. Such fairness perceptions can influence employees' attitudes and behavior for good or bad, resulting in positive or negative effect on the employees' as well as organization's performance. More specifically, it involves the ways in which employee perceives whether they have been treated fairly on their jobs and the ways in which those perceptions influence other work related variables (Moorman, 1991). The study of distributive justice saw its origin in Adam's equity theory (1965) which states that people were concerned not about the level of outcome but the fairness of those outcomes. The fairness of outcomes can be determined by calculating the ratio of contribution (i.e., inputs) to the outcomes and then compare that ratio with other's ratio. There could be many instances of distributive injustice, for example, employees may feel that there has been unfair distribution of pay, work load, rewards, recognition, etc. and such outcomes are not according to their efforts and contribution. As a result, unsatisfied employees will reduce their subsequent efforts which are detrimental to both – the employee as well as the organization. Procedural justice is referred as the fairness of procedures leading to a particular outcome. Procedural justice can outweigh distributive justice i.e., people may be willing to accept an unwanted outcome if they believe that decision leading to that outcome was conducted according to organizational justice principles. Procedural justice affects what employees believe about the organization as a whole. If the process is perceived as fair and unbiased, employees show greater loyalty and more willingness to behave as well as contribute in an organization's best interests. They are also less likely to deceive the organization and its leaders. Moorman, Blakely and Niehoff (1998) suggested that actions designed to promote procedural fairness may be useful in communicating how a company values and supports its employees. Employees' perception of a fair decision process can be judged by criteria such as voice, consistency, neutrality, accuracy, representativeness, morality and ethicality. Interactional justice refers to the quality of interpersonal treatment received by employees particularly as part of formal decision making procedures. The interactional justice was introduced by Bies and Moag (1986) during a study of expectations for inter- personal treatment during recruitment and they identified four criteria for interactional justice. The four criteria include, justification (i.e., explaining the basis for decisions), truthfulness (i.e., being candid and not engaging in deception), respect (i.e., being polite rather than rude) and propriety (i.e., refraining from improper remarks or prejudicial statements). A large number of studies have sought to link justice perceptions to a variety of organizational outcomes including job satisfaction, organizational commitment, withdrawal and citizenship behaviours (Colquitt, Wesson, Porter & Ng, 2001). Sheppard, Lewicki and Minton (1992) stated that 'equitable pay improves individual performance, equal treatment raises group spirit, voice creates commitment to a decision and access creates a loyal ally'. It is needless to emphasize that committed and loyal employees will produce highest quality of customer services leading to overall customer satisfaction culminating into organizational success.

(b) **Work-Life Balance:** Work-life balance has been defined as 'satisfaction and good functioning at work and at home with a minimum of role conflict' (Clark, 2000) or in simpler terms, it is the balance of an individual's levels of work and private life. Work-life balance involves having sufficient time for all type of experiences such as career, family, friends, community, and leisure pursuits. A number of factors are responsible that have increased the pressure of work in today's competitive work environment such as advances in information technology, importance of high quality customer service, organizations' need for constant availability and the pace of change and adjustment, which consumes employees' valuable time that could, for instance, be spent with the family (Guest, 2002). Additionally, changes in the structure of the workforce, such as an increased demand on working hours, a larger number of women joining the workforce, and many more couples involved in the workforce in order to fulfill their financial commitments further warranted the need for HR policies to provide employees with opportunities to improve their balance between work and private life. Organizations, therefore, implement various work-life benefits or policies and family – friendly practices such as flexible work hours, childcare programmes, flexible leave, reducing work hours, part-time jobs, compressed work week, telecommuting, etc. to help employees well manage their different fronts including personal well-being, professional development, and family responsibilities. A healthy balance between family and job leads to higher job satisfaction, thereby reducing the cost to organization and enhancing employee performance (Kanwar, Singh & Kodwani, 2009).

7. **Organizational Development:** The concept of organizational development (OD) has emerged to help the planned change for organizational effectiveness and it concentrates on dimensions such as norms, values, attitudes, relationships, organizational climate, etc. Organization development is an effort, which is planned, organization-wide, and managed from the top, to increase organization effectiveness and health through planned interventions in the organization's "processes," using behavioral-science knowledge (Beckhard, 1969). OD efforts are intended to develop systemic changes that are long lasting and are aimed at developing an organization's process competencies to increase their `enabling' capabilities. An organization development intervention is a sequence of activities, actions, and events intended to help an organization improve its performance and effectiveness. Intervention design, or action planning, derives from careful diagnosis and is meant to resolve specific problems and to improve particular areas of organizational functioning identified in the diagnosis (Cummings & Worley, 2009). The most important OD mechanisms or interventions include survey feedback, process consultation, sensitivity training, goal setting and planning, the management grid, team building, management-by-objectives, job enrichment, changes in organizational structure, participative management, quality circles (Rao, 2008). The culture created through OD efforts may be able to nurture development of human resources (Rao & Abraham, 1986). All the three units of a work system i.e., individual employees, group/teams and the organizations are benefitted by the OD programmes and such benefits include performance improvement, job satisfaction and self-

change. OD programmes encourage teamwork, communication skills, cooperation, interpersonal relations, openness, etc. OD efforts broadly aim at improving the organizational effectiveness and job satisfaction of the employees that can be achieved by humanizing the organizations and encouraging the personal growth of individual employees.

CHAPTER 2

HRD as an Integrated System

It is widely accepted that measurement of HRD interventions is necessary because it would help the organization to know how well they are serving the purpose for which interventions are made and the area that need strengthening. It is therefore worthwhile to measure the effectiveness of HRD systems in organizations as it gives an idea about the level of existence of HRD interventions being implemented and the areas that need further improvement. While reviewing various HRD frameworks, it was observed that although certain individual HRD practices are viewed as superior to others, however, a single superior HRD practice without other supporting practices and mechanisms in the system is inadequate as a driver of sustainable performance outcomes. Further, successful implementation of HRD involves taking an integral look and making efforts to use as many mechanisms as possible (Rao & Abraham, 1986). Consequently, it is proposed that an integrated system of HRD dimensions as presented in Figure 2.1 that includes developmental climate, performance appraisal, employee training, employee empowerment, quality of work life (with focus on organizational justice and work-life balance) will provide an assessment of overall HRD effectiveness and also produce desirable effects on employee attitudes and behaviours. Mc Donald & Hite (2005) claimed that HRD can make a difference in individuals' careers by attending to important organizational support mechanisms such as fairness and equity, environmental issues, and life-work balance. As these career support mechanisms are included individually, career development practice is not integrated in the proposition of this text. In addition, organizational development being a long term initiative to induce change is also not included in this text.

Fig. 2.1: HRD as an Integrated System

Theoretical Framework

HRD subsystems have becoming more broader and indefinite due to changes in the way an organization perceives their effectiveness and efficacy, and so the studies on HRD were found abundant but distributed with different subsystems or practices addressed either individually or in different combinations.

The HRD climate was measured as general climate, OCTAPACE culture and HRD mechanisms in an empirical study by Mittal (2013). OCTAPACE culture includes dimensions of openness, confrontation, trust, autonomy, pro-action, authenticity, collaboration and experimentation. Primary data were collected from 200 employees belonging to a public sector bank and a private sector bank through a structured questionnaire developed by Rao and Abraham (1986). The results of the study revealed that the perceptions towards the general HRD climate and HRD mechanisms in public sector bank (SBI) was found better as compared to private sector bank (Axis bank). However, no significant difference was found as regards to the OCTAPACE culture of the two study banks. Kilam and Kumari (2012) conducted an exploratory study to assess the current status of career planning and HRD in Indian public sector banks. The investigators also attempted to find the relative significance of other HRD sub-systems. Data were collected from 201 managers from fifteen public sector banks in India through a structured questionnaire designed specifically for the study. The results of the study revealed that career planning & development was perceived to be one of the most important HRD sub-systems and not the most important HRD sub-system; training and development was found as the most important HRD subsystem. Majority of respondents believed that public sector banks are HRD oriented only to some extent and there is much scope for HRD orientation in public sector banks. Most of the respondents recognized that banking organizations and their environment have supported the employees in their career growth. It was also found that around 81% of respondents perceived that well-established corporate sector in India and the foreign banks had better career planning and HRD system as compared to Indian public sector banks. Jain and Premkumar (2011) conducted an exploratory research to study the HRD practices in Indian Organizations. The main objectives of the study were: a) to study the HRD practices in Indian organizations; b) to study the concern of various stakeholders for the cause of HRD and to measure their impact on HRD practices; c) to study the common management practices and to measure their impact on HRD practices; d) to study the effectiveness of human resources in terms of their 'Productivity'; and e) to study the impact of HRD practices on the 'Productivity' of human resources in Indian organizations. The sub-systems of HRD practices included functioning of HRD department, concern of top and senior executives for the cause of HRD, capabilities and concerns of HRD managers, employee communication, employee training, performance appraisal, job enrichment, career planning, employee empowerment. The study was based on the cross-section perceptual analysis of a sample size of 300 executives from public as well as private sector industries and manufacturing as well as service industries in India. Measures used in the study were: HRD practices scale developed by Kandula (2001), HRD facilitators scale developed by Kandula (2001), Management Styles questionnaire developed by Khandwalla (1995) and Human resource effectiveness scale developed by the researchers. The study found that HRD practices with reference to functioning of HRD department, employees' training, performance appraisal, job enrichment and career planning were moderately effective whereas employee communication and employee empowerment were found less effective across the various sectors of Indian organizations. All the selected HRD sub-systems were found to be positively correlated with one another and high degree of positive correlation was found between employee communication and employee empowerment and job enrichment and employee empowerment. The investigators also found that the various stakeholders including top and senior executives, line managers and supervisors and individual employees and employee unions all have moderate concerns for HRD cause without any significant variation between the public and private sectors as well as manufacturing and service organizations. Results of regression and correlation analyses also indicated that the selected four management styles viz., participative, altruistic, organic and professional were found to be practiced to moderate extent across the sectors and have high positive correlation with one another and have significant impact on productivity of human resources. The study also concluded that all the above HRD sub-systems have significant impact on the productivity of human resources. Solkhe and Chaudhary (2011) conducted an empirical study to determine the impact of HRD climate, OCTAPAC culture on job satisfaction as an organizational performance measure in the selected public sector enterprises located in North India. The HRD climate questionnaire developed by Rao and Abraham (1986) was used to measure the extent to which a development climate exists in the study organizations. Job satisfaction was measured using a 19-items scale. Data were collected from 71 managers from various departments and different hierarchical levels of the organization. The mean scores indicated that employees in this organization are helpful to each other and are very informal and do not hesitate to discuss their personal problems with their supervisors. The results of the study indicated that senior managers in this organization believe that employee behaviour can be changed and people can be developed at any stage of their life. It was also found that company is having a reasonable level of development orientation and employees are contended with the same. But the employees were quite unsatisfied with respect to the promotion decisions in the company. Among the OCTAPAC values (openness, confrontation, trust, autonomy, pro-action, authenticity and collaboration), it was found that employees in the organization trust each other and they were not afraid to express or discuss the feelings with their subordinates, they confront their problem rather than accusing each other behind the back. It was observed that people are happy with the work and the organization in general. In regression analysis, it was found that 61% of the variance in job satisfaction is explained by the HRD climate variables. This finding indicated that HRD climate has a definite impact on job satisfaction which in turn leads to the increased organizational performance. Chaudhary, Rangnekar and Barua (2011) conducted an empirical study to explore the impact of HRD climate on employee engagement with reference to both private and public sector as well as manufacturing and service firms in India. The study was conducted on 85 business executives from both private and public sector manufacturing and service firms in India. Work Engagement Scale (Schaufeli et al., 2002) was used to measure employee engagement. The scale consisted of three sub-scales; absorption, vigour and dedication. HRD climate was measured using the HRD climate survey questionnaire developed by Rao and Abraham (1986) with the items categorized under three dimensions;

general climate, HRD mechanisms and OCTAPACE culture. Data were analyzed using correlation and regression analysis. The results of the study revealed that both HRD climate and employee engagement in the organizations under study were found at a moderate level. Out of the three dimensions of HRD climate, the mean average score of "The successful implementation of HRD mechanisms" was found to be highest followed by general HRD climate and OCTAPACE culture was found to have the lowest average mean score. Thus, HRD mechanisms dimension is more prevalent than the other two. Results of correlation analysis indicate that HRD climate and all its dimensions were positively and significantly correlated with employee engagement. The general climate dimension of HRD climate was the most significant predictor of employee engagement followed by the HRD mechanism dimension, however, OCTAPACE culture's impact was found to be insignificant. As a result, the authors opined that in order to improve the engagement level of the employees, HR departments should attempt to improve the HRD climate of their organizations specially the support from top management and line managers and through fair and successful implementation of the HRD mechanisms like career planning, performance appraisal, training, job rotation and potential appraisal. Authors further suggested that fair performance appraisal and feedback should be provided to the employees fostering learning and growth of the employees. Appreciating good performance helps boost up the confidence of employees and enhances their motivational level resulting in them giving their heart and soul to work resulting in enhanced engagement levels. Saraswathi (2010) in an empirical study assessed the extent of HRD climate prevailing in manufacturing and software organizations in India and made a comparison between the HRD climate of these two types of organizations. HRD climate questionnaire developed by Rao and Abraham (1986) was used to measure general climate, OCTAPAC culture and HRD mechanisms. Data were collected from 100 employees from different software and manufacturing organizations in India. The study concluded that all the three dimensions of HRD climate were found better in software organizations as compared to the manufacturing organizations. The study also revealed that in both types of organizations, training was found better implemented followed by performance appraisal and feedback, potential appraisal and career planning, and rewards and employee welfare. Saxena and Tiwari (2009) conducted an empirical study to find out the type of HRD climate that is prevailing in public sector banks in Ahmedabad. Banks were selected on the basis of judgmental sampling and respondents on the basis of non-probability random sampling. Data were collected from 90 employees of three public sector banks using HRD climate questionnaire (5-point likert type scale) developed by Rao and Abraham (1986). Data analysis indicated that the HRD climate in public sector banks was found at average level. It was also found that the perception of employees regarding the HRD climate do not differ significantly on the basis of gender, qualification and designation but it differs significantly on the basis of age. Purang (2008) conducted an empirical study to measure the HRD climate and its relationship with the organizational commitment in Indian organizations. Ten dimensions of HRD climate was studied, namely, participation, succession planning, human resource information, organization development, training, appraisal, counselling, career planning, reward and welfare and job enrichment. The technique of purposive sampling was adopted in selecting the five organizations so that all three types of organizations i.e., public, private and multinational could be studied to allow for a comparative analysis between three types of banks. Data were collected using HRD climate questionnaire with 27 items developed by Daftaur (1996) from 247 middle managers randomly selected across various functions in the five organizations. Data analysis from the responses of 247 middle level managers in five organizations revealed that there exists a positive relationship between the dimensions of HRD climate and organizational commitment of managers and specifically four dimensions of HRD climate viz., career planning, performance appraisal, job enrichment and organization development were found to be strong predictors of organizational commitment. Rao, Rao and Yadav (2007) examined the current status of structuring of the HRD function and HRD sub-systems in India against the "Integrated HRD System Framework" proposed by Pareek and Rao (1975). HRD audit of 12 organizations representing a variety of Indian corporates was conducted with the use of questionnaires, interviews, company documents, observation, secondary data, etc. indicated that HRD function is not well structured, is inadequately differentiated, poorly staffed, and fails to meet the requirements of integrated HRD systems framework. The HRD subsystems, however, have evolved and matured to a substantial degree, especially the performance management system, and training and development system. Organization development and feedback and counseling are in the next level of maturity. Potential appraisal and career planning and development are the least developed and least used sub-systems. Finally, the authors concluded that the HRD departments need to have professionally trained and competent staff, and if they have to make an impact, they should enhance the maturity levels of all the sub-systems of HRD. Purang (2006) made a survey to measure and compare the HRD climate perceptions of middle level managers from five Indian organizations; two private sectors, two public sectors and one multinational organization. Ten dimensions of HRD climate were studied, namely, participation, succession planning, human resource information, organization development, training, appraisal, counselling, career planning, reward and welfare and job enrichment. The technique of purposive sampling was adopted in selecting the five organizations so that all three types of organizations i.e., public, private and multinational could be studied to allow for a comparative analysis between three types of banks. Data were collected using HRD climate questionnaire with 27 items developed by Daftaur (1996) from 247 middle managers randomly selected across various functions in the five organizations. Data analysis indicated that the employee perceptions regarding the human resource development climate were found significantly better in the private sector and multinational organizations in comparison to the public sector organization. Based on their findings, authors suggested that public sector banks should improve the HRD climate prevalent in their organizations and focus on various HR policies and practices like encouraging active employee involvement and interaction in the day to day functioning, training, appraisal and reward mechanisms. Priyadarshini and Venkatapathy (2003) in an empirical study measured the extent of HRD practices and organizational effectiveness as well as the impact of HRD practices on organizational effectiveness in the nationalized and private sector banks belonging to large and small category based on their deposits. The extent of HRD practices was measured through a 87-item human resource development questionnaire (HRDQ) based on four-point likert type scale developed by the researchers (1996) that elicit the extent to which the various HRD dimensions such as role analysis, induction, performance appraisal, potential appraisal, performance counseling, career planning, training, quality of work life and organization development, are practiced in organizations. Organizational effectiveness was measured with the help of 99-items organizational effectiveness questionnaire (OEQ) developed by Venkatapathy and Priyadarshini (2001). The OEQ measures the following dimensions of organizational effectiveness: immediate supervision, management leadership, compensation, feedback and growth, working conditions and job demands, perceptions of quality, communication, productivity and decision making, personal morale and motivation and organizational values. Indian banks rated as top and low performers for the year 2001 as per Business Today's 'Best Banks 2001' was the population for the study. Out of such rated banks, 20 top performing and 20 low performing banks operating in Coimbatore constituted the sampling frame. These banks were further categorized into nationalized and private banks in each of the categories based on their ownership. Data were collected from randomly selected 200 managers of nationalized and private sector banks. Results of ANOVA revealed that private sector banks were found to have weaker HRD practices as compared to nationalized banks. Hence, they must strengthen their HRD practices. Further, it was found that top performing banks have a high extent of HRD practices in their organizations which influences the effectiveness of their organizations. It was also found that HRD practices in the organizations have impact on the effectiveness of organizations and hence on their performance irrespective of their size and ownership. Based on these findings, researchers recommended that low performing banks as well as private sector banks must strengthen their HRD practices in order to improve their performance.

The sum of the earlier research works clearly reflects that a number of studies have been carried out by previous researchers on various aspects of HRD sub-systems and organizational performance outcomes such as productivity, job satisfaction, turnover intentions, employee engagement, organizational commitment and organizational citizenship behaviour. While a number of previous research studies have focused on specific HRD sub-systems either in isolation or in combination, none of them addressed the development focussed bundles of practices like performance appraisal, employee training, employee empowerment, organizational justice and work-life balance alongwith general HRD climate in an integrated form.

CHAPTER 3

HRD Climate

The success of HRD in any organization depends, to a large extent on the existence of a favourable HRD climate. The policies, procedures, culture and structure, all together, decides the extent to which employees are satisfied in an organization and ultimately influences their attitudes, behaviours and overall performance.

Definition

HRD Climate is the supportive climate that is essential for proper implementation of HRD practices. It can be characterized by tendencies such as treating employees as the most important resources, perceiving that developing employees is the job of every manager, believing in the capability of employees, communicating openly, encouraging risk taking, making efforts to help employees recognize their strengths and weaknesses, creating a general climate of trust, collaboration and autonomy, supportive personnel policies, and supportive HRD practices.

Theoretical Framework

Studies on HRD climate in Indian organizations have emphasized on human resource interventions and improvement of organizational synergy as strategies for better and healthier climate (Singh, 1998; Pattanayak, 2000). Rao and Abraham (1986) conducted HRD climate survey for the first time in India and reported an average HRD climate in Indian organizations. Better HRD climate was found in software companies as compared to manufacturing organizations (Saraswathi, 2010) while in public sector banks average HRD climate was reported by Saxena and Tiwari (2009). Srimannarayan (2007) conducted an empirical study in Dubai-based organizations and found that banking sector had favourable HRD climate as compared to insurance, shipping, trading and food industry. Mishra and Bhardwaj (2002) concluded that the HRD climate in a private sector undertaking in India was good. A moderate level of HRD climate was reported by Srimannarayan (2008) in Indian organizations covering manufacturing, service and IT sectors. Mittal (2013) found that the perceptions of employees towards HRD climate was found better in public sector bank (SBI) than private sector bank (Axis bank). Kumar (2005) found that organizational climate (OC) of new private sector banks and foreign banks in India was perceived as significantly better as compared to public sector banks. The difference was seen on leadership, motivation, communication, interaction influence, decision making, goal setting, and control process aspects of OC. In a study conducted by Chandrashekhar in 2009, a positive and significant relationship was found between HRD climate and employee engagement. HRD climate was found to be positively correlated with individual efficiency, organizational efficiency and productivity (Jain, Singhal & Singh, 1997). Agarwala (2002) found significantly high correlation between HRD climate and an extent of satisfaction with the implementation of innovative HR practices. Rodrigues and Chincholkar (2005) found no significant difference between the HRD climate of engineering institute and public sector, although HRDC of engineering institute was found to be comparatively weaker. Purang (2006) found out that in order to improve the productivity of the employees in the organization it is important to focus on various aspects of the HRD climate prevalent in the organization. HRD climate was found to be a strong predictor of organizational commitment, job satisfaction, attitude and role efficacy. Chaudhary, Rangnekar and Barua (2011) reported that the general climate dimension of HRD climate was the most significant predictor of employee engagement followed by the HRD mechanism dimension, however, OCTAPACE culture's impact was found to be insignificant. The above review of literature clearly indicates that HRD climate play a significant role in the successful performance of organizations. Most of the studies on HRD climate invariably conceptualized HRD climate under three dimensions of general climate, OCTAPACE culture and implementation of HRD mechanisms. The general climate deals with the importance given to human resources development in general by the top management and line managers. The OCTAPACE items deal with the extent to which openness, confrontation, trust, autonomy, proactivity, authenticity, collaboration and experimentation are valued and promoted in the organization. HRD mechanisms measure the extent to which various HRD mechanisms like potential appraisal, performance appraisal, training and development, career planning and development etc. are implemented seriously and successfully.

Elements of HRD Climate

(i) **Supportive HR policies:** The effective HRD climate depends to a great extent on the organizational policies that emphasize employee development. Thus, In order to promote a real HRD climate in any organization, it is imperative to have the prevalence of general supportive climate not only by dint of the support and commitment of the top management and line management but immensely good supportive personnel policies and positive attitudes are equally important towards such development.

(ii) **Organizational support:** Organizational support represents employee perceptions that their organizations have a developmental environment where employees are encouraged in developing themselves by acquiring new knowledge and skills and low job performers are helped to acquire competence rather than being left unattended. It is important to study organizational support because it is employee's perceptions of organizational environment that may lead to expected attitudinal and behavioral responses.

(iii) **Supervisor support:** Another important work environment variable is supervisor support. Support represents employee perceptions that their superiors will be tolerant and allows them to learn from their mistakes. Employees expect their superiors to take active interest in their development and provide them with assistance when needed. When employees receive support from superiors, they tend to feel more content with their jobs.

(iv) **Teamwork:** Teamwork reflects that people work together and use one another's skills to achieve a common goal. Such collaborative attitude encourages employees to help others and ask for help from others. It develops team spirit and manages a friendly and open climate in the organization. It increases productivity of individual as well as the organization; motivate joint decision and participative approach, proper utilization of resources and better quality of products and services.

(v) **Trust:** Trust is taking people at their face value and believing what they say. It indicates that employees, departments, and groups trust each other and can be relied upon to do whatever they say they will do. It also includes maintaining the confidentiality of information shared by others, so that nobody can misuse it. Trust within the employees to the management and management's trust on employees result in high level of empathy, coordination among employees, friendly and disciplined atmosphere and higher productivity.

(vi) **Openness in Communication:** Openness in communication is present when the employees feel free to discuss their ideas, activities, problems and feelings with each other. Openness promotes free interaction, feedback and discussion between management and employees as well as among employees, thereby help in creating a climate conducive for the development of employees.

CHAPTER 4

Performance Appraisal System

Performance appraisal system (PAS) has been a key organizational process for the management and the development of personnel. Performance appraisals are considered to be most essential element in creating positive work environment and involve a range of attributes, such as reward, communication, feedback, employee reactions, equity and fairness, trust and acceptance, attitudes towards conflict, and social context. Performance appraisal (PA) are activities through which organizations seek to assess employees and develop their competence, enhance performance and distribute rewards.

Definition

Performance Appraisal is the process of identifying, evaluating and developing the work performance of employees in the organization, so that the organizational goals and objectives are more effectively achieved, while at the same time benefiting employees in terms of recognition, receiving feedback, catering for work and offering career guidance (Lansbury, 1988). It assists in evaluating an employee's current or past performance relative to his or her performance standards.

Theoretical Framework

It is necessary to address employees' reactions toward their performance appraisal for many reasons, including (a) the notion that reactions represent a criterion of great interest to practitioners and (b) the fact that reactions have been theoretically linked to determinants of appraisal acceptance and success but have been relatively ignored in research (Keeping & Levy, 2000). Earlier researchers have claimed that in order for performance appraisal to positively influence employee behaviour and future development, employees must experience positive appraisal reactions to important aspects of the appraisal process (Bernardin & Beatty 1984;

Murphy & Cleveland, 1995; Kuvaas, 2006). Appraisal reactions such as satisfaction, acceptability, and motivation to use feedback, are cited as an important trend in the appraisal research during the past ten years (Levy & Williams, 2004). Erdogan (2002) suggest that performance appraisal can make important contribution to effective human resource management, and eventually organizational performance. Employee performance has, therefore, been identified as a crucial determinant of success in all the business sectors and hence there is a growing interest in the effective management of employee performance.

Extant literature has shown that there is a critical link that exists between satisfaction with appraisal processes and appraisal effectiveness (Bernardin & Beatty, 1984; Dobbins, Cardy, & Platz- Vieno, 1990). Dipboye & de Pontbriand (1981) showed that employees were more satisfied and had greater acceptance of PA when employee development and performance improvement were emphasized in it. Jain and Kamble (2005) pointed out that the effectiveness of performance appraisal system is based on the extent to which the system is HRD oriented. Well-structured appraisals should directly relate to noted improvements in any weak areas (Broady-Preston & Steel, 2002). The benefits of an effective appraisal scheme lie in the fact that it leads to improved performance throughout the organizations (Fisher, 1996). Studies on employee's reactions to appraisals and feedback (e.g., Taylor, Masterson, Renard, & Tracy, 1998) suggested the outcome of appraisal in improving employee performance. The perceptions of fairness influence the way people think, feel, and act on the job (Bies & Shapiro 1987), thereby influencing positive affective reactions like performance appraisal satisfaction (Thurston, 2001; Cook & Crossman, 2004). Feedback from the performance review should be used as a basis for development and improvement. Research has shown that effective feedback does improve employee performance (Latting, 1992). Further, if participants do not perceive the system to be fair, the feedback to be accurate, or sources to be credible, then they are more likely to ignore and not use the feedback they receive (Facteau et al., 1998). In an empirical study of 163 BPO employees, Monis and Shreedhara (2010) found that objectivity in the appraisals, the accuracy of the previous appraisals and viewing appraisals as a motivating tool have emerged as the significant variables and all these three variables are positively associated with the satisfaction of the respondents towards the performance appraisal system. Employees demonstrate higher level of commitment when they perceive that performance appraisal is associated with employee development (Lee & Bruvold, 2003). In their recent review of PA research, Levy and Williams (2004) called for more field research on the relationship between PA reactions and employee attitudes and behaviour. They claimed that an appraisal system will be ineffective if ratees (and raters) do not see it as fair, useful, valid, accurate, etc. If ratees are dissatisfied or perceive a system as unfair, they will be less likely to use evaluations as feedback to improve their performance (Ilgen, Fisher, & Taylor, 1979). Jawahar (2006) investigated the potential predictors and consequences of satisfaction with performance appraisal feedback and found that satisfaction with rater and previous performance ratings influence employees' satisfaction with performance appraisal feedback. Shrivastava and Purang (2012) found that older employees have performance expectations that are well set, better clarified, have greater confidence in their raters and feel they are provided more feedback, rating decision are explained in a fair manner and are treated in a respectable way whereas in case of private sector bank employees, as age increases they do not feel their expectations are well set and clarified. Measuring appraisal effectiveness involves, among other things, assessing perceptions of or actual rater errors and biases, rating accuracy and reactions of raters and ratees about the PA system in place (Keeping & Levy, 2000). They further claimed that satisfaction with performance appraisal is the most frequently measured appraisal reaction.

An effective PA system must include the use of valid and reliable appraisal instruments for the collection of relevant and useful appraisal data upon which necessary HR decisions could be based (Agbola, Hemans & Abena, 2011). In order to measure employee's job performance, appraisal instruments are based on various methods such as graphic rating scales, forced distributions, ranking methods, BARS or MBO. As regards to frequency of appraisal, researchers have claimed that in order for performance appraisals to be effective in dynamic and changing environment, the process must be ongoing and frequent (Letham & Wexeley, 1998; Mullins, 2005). Fisher (1994) noted that the modal frequency of appraisal review is annual. It has been found that raters play a crucial role in the success and failure of any appraisal system (Pooyan & Eberhardt 1989). Performance appraisal usually involves 'evaluating performance based on the judgments and opinions of subordinates, peers, supervisors, other managers and even workers themselves' (Jackson & Schuler, 2003). Thus, typically, an employee first completes self-appraisal and then his/her performance is evaluated by immediate supervisor or manager and then the performance is further reviewed by senior managers in the hierarchy and finally forwarded to HR manager for processing. Self-appraisals may be useful in enhancing the developmental and motivational impact of evaluation and may promote increased commitment to performance goals and better acceptance of criticism (Campbell & Lee, 1988; Riggio & Cole, 1992). However, many organizations use multiple raters for performance evaluation. Using multiple rating sources in performance appraisals provides unique perspectives on performance that are available from different sources (e.g., supervisors, peers, subordinates, customers, etc.) that are often ignored by traditional performance appraisal.

All managers who currently conduct performance appraisals or who would potentially do so must be given proper training on how to conduct performance appraisals (Kondrasuk, 2011). Such training may involve the aspects of PA process, policies, objectivity, evaluation criteria, use of appraisal instrument, psychological concerns, legal aspects, use of results, etc. Schraeder, Becton, and Portis (2007) proposed that training should be provided to improve raters' ability to produce accurate and reliable evaluations. Wanguri (1995) suggested that training in the proper use of rating instrument is essential in order to minimize rating error. Researchers (Bernardin & Buckley, 1984; Murphy & Balzer, 1989) have shown that rater-error training (e.g., training that familiarizes raters with common errors and provides suggestions on how to avoid them) results in reducing common rating errors. Further, training that focuses on techniques that raters can use to observe, store, recall, and use performance information has been shown to increase accuracy (Heneman, 1988; Pelly & Dossett, 1991). Researchers have also proposed that rating errors can be reduced significantly and that accuracy can be improved as a result of rater training, regardless of the rating scale used (Fay & Latham, 1982; Regel & Hollmann, 1987). New employees, as a part of induction program, should also be educated on how their performance will be measured, monitored and evaluated. Thus, proper training and education of those involved in the PA process can contribute to an effective PA system.

Elements of Performance Appraisal System

(i) **Performance Improvement:** It indicates improvement in an employee's job performance

(ii) **Employee Development:** It refers to employee competence development in terms of development of knowledge, skills and attitudes to enable him/her for performing better not only in existing job but also for future tasks and assignments.

(iii) **Fairness in PA Rating:** When the rating provided after the completion of PA process is devoid of any bias and subjectivity, it is said to be fair rating. It indicates that the procedure used to evaluate an employee's performance is fair.

(iv) **Accuracy of PA Rating:** It indicates that the rating given to employees is actually based on their efforts, abilities and performance during the appraisal period rather than any bias, favouritism or rating error (such as halo effect, central tendency error, recency effect, leniency or strictness effect, etc.). It also indicates that an employee's performance rating is based on some pre-set standards of performance.

(v) **Providing Feedback:** It refers to providing information about the level of achievement in relation to pre-defined performance standards and behavior of employees during the performance period and to prescribe the ways for taking appropriate actions in the future. Such information helps to review past performance of employees, rectifying performance deficiencies and to set new standards of work, if required.

(vi) **Explaining Rating Decisions:** It refers to clear communication and justification of rating decisions made as a result of PA process. It involves open discussions between the appraiser and employee about the reasons of positive or negative deviations from the pre-set objectives.

(vii) **Overall Satisfaction with PA system:** This indicates overall satisfaction with performance appraisal system being practiced and includes its factors viz., policy, design, development, implementation and use of appraisal outcomes.

CHAPTER 5

Employee Empowerment

In today's highly competitive marketplace, HR professionals and managers must ensure that 'people practices' of their organizations are designed to give employees the skills, capabilities and motivation to win over in every situation. One way to achieve this objective is to empower employees for optimum performance and job satisfaction. Employees should be empowered because it is through empowerment that an organization will develop a culture which reflects employee commitment in order to survive, grow, compete, and face challenges posed by globalization with confidence (Sahoo, Behera & Tripathy, 2010).

Definition

Employee Empowerment is a process of orienting and enabling individuals to think, behave and take action in an autonomous way. It helps the workers to own their work and take responsibility for their results. Empowerment has been examined according to two separate approaches - structural or relational empowerment, which focuses on redesigned management practices, and psychological or motivational empowerment, which emphasizes an individual's psychological enabling.

Theoretical Framework

Empowerment is thought to leave employees optimistic, involved, committed, able to cope with adversity, and willing to perform independently and responsibly. According to Kanter (1983), the mandate of management is to create conditions for work effectiveness by ensuring employees to have access to the information, support, and resources necessary to accomplish work and is provided ongoing opportunities for development. This results in increased levels of organizational commitment, feelings of autonomy, and self-efficacy. Thus, empowerment is a process of enhancing feelings of self-efficacy among organizational members through the identification of conditions that foster powerlessness and through their removal by both formal organizational practices and informal techniques of providing efficacy information (Conger & Kanungo, 1988). According to Hardy and Leiba-O'Sullivan (1998), employee empowerment is the latest variation of practices such as employee involvement and participation in organizational decision-making, which have its roots in industrial democracy. Throughout the empowerment literature, it may be found that employee empowerment is being studied from two different approaches (e.g., Koberg, Boss, Senjem, & Goodman, 1999; Liden & Arad, 1996; Spreitzer, 1995; Thomas & Veltbouse, 1990): (a) Structural or relational empowerment, and (b) Psychological or motivational empowerment. Structural empowerment is defined as redesigned structures or management practices wherein superiors distribute responsibility and information to their subordinates, as well as allow employees to participate in decision-making processes (Cho & Faerman, 2010). According to Menon (2001), structural empowerment is a traditional approach and it focuses on the actions of 'power-holders' who transfer some power to the less powerful, but it does not address the psychological state of those being empowered. He further argued that to achieve an adequate understanding of empowerment processes it is important to consider the "perspective of the individual employee". The psychological dimension of empowerment moves away from the traditional study of management practices and instead emphasizes employees' perceptions (Peccei & Rosenthal, 2001). Through such an approach, the emphasis is upon perceptions and beliefs of power, competence, control and self-efficacy (Psoinos & Smithson, 2002). Evolving from the Bandura's (1977) concept of self- efficacy, Conger and Kanungo (1988) defined psychological empowerment as "a process whereby an individual's belief in his or her self-efficacy is enhanced" and argue that motivational approaches to empowerment are related to self-efficacy. Thus, structural empowerment focuses on the factors of the situation in which people work, whereas psychological empowerment focuses on a subjective assessment of how people feel as they perform their work.

Empowerment is an umbrella term in the literature often used to indicate different factors. Burke (1986) equated empowerment to delegation while Thomas and Velthouse (1990) used the term to indicate internal psychological state of the individual. In their conceptualization, Thomas and Velthouse (1990) described empowerment as a set of four cognitions reflecting an employee's orientation to his/her role in terms of meaning (i.e., the value of his or her work), competence (i.e., his or her capability to perform the work), self-determination (i.e., choice in initiating and regulating actions), and impact (the ability to affect or influence organizational outcomes). The competence factor is similar to Conger and Kanungo's (1988) concept of self-efficacy. Later, Spreitzer (1995) examined measures of these four components and her confirmatory factor analysis supported that empowerment belief or 'psychological' empowerment is the higher-order factor and each of the four cognitions as distinguished components. Bogler and Somech (2004) identified six dimensions of empowerment such as: decision-making, professional growth, status, self-efficacy, autonomy and impact. Yukl and Becker (2006) have outlined a few facilitators for effective empowerment: informal organizational structure; flexible, participative and learning culture; reward and recognition system; non-routine and challenging jobs; access to resources and funds; degree of autonomy and selection of leader; leader as a role model; and mutual trust. Wilkinson (1998) identified five types of empowerment: information sharing, upward problem solving, task autonomy, attitudinal shaping, and self-management. Empowerment can be viewed from two approaches, first employees may `be' empowered by organizational interventions such as participative decision making or increased job autonomy (e.g., Hackman & Oldham, 1980), and secondly, employees may `feel' empowered on the basis of their perceptions and beliefs of self- efficacy (e.g., Conger & Kanungo, 1988; Parker & Price, 1994). Bowen and Lawler (1995) emphasizes the need for high-involvement practices that create in employees an `empowered state of mind' while Argyris (1998, 2000) underscored internal commitment and personal employee reasons and motivation.

Sparrow and Budhwar (1997) questioned 137 Indian personnel directors regarding their attitudes towards a variety of practices and policies commonly associated with HRM. Out of nine clusters of HRM characteristics, Indian managers attached the least value to 'structural empowerment'. In a cross-country study, Diwedi (2000) found that the perceived level of empowerment in different work organizations in India and Philippines was at a moderate level and that there was no difference in the two countries as regards to the perceived level of empowerment. Bhatnagar (2005) focused on psychological empowerment in a study of 607 Indian managers and found it as a strong predictor of organizational commitment. Chaudhary, Rangnekar & Barua (2011) in a study of Indian executives reported that occupational self-efficacy (which is conceptualized as dimension of psychological self-efficacy in our study) is a strong predictor of employee engagement. In a study of 288 Indian managers, Bhatnagar and Sharma (2004) found the presence of psychological empowerment at a moderate level. As evident, hardly any of the Indian studies addressed an integrated form of empowerment that focused on structural as well as psychological approach. Even a good number of the western studies have concluded that most of the empirical research to date has taken empowerment as an individual level psychological experience (e.g., Raub & Robert, 2013; Spreitzer, Kizilos & Nason, 1997), while little to no research has been conducted recently on empowerment as a macro construct reflecting managerial structures and practices (Seibert, Silver & Randolph, 2004).

Based on these findings from the earlier studies, it may be argued that the true nature of empowerment can be better examined by integrating the two different approaches i.e., by focusing on organizational practices and also on psychological state of individual employee. After a careful review of existing literature on empowerment, an integrative perspective on employee empowerment is developed, combining structural as well as psychological empowerment factors. Structural empowerment will be defined as the involvement or participation in the decision- making process (Pardo & Lloyd, 2003), allowing the employees to participate in planning and decision making and keeping them informed about what is going on in the organization. Following Vasugi, Kaviatha and Prema (2011) and Chisholm and Vansina's (1993) emphasis on participation as a key element of empowerment, the present book considered participative decision-making as the measure of structural empowerment. Considering the concluding suggestion of Conger and Kanungo (1988) that self-efficacy should be operationalized and tested in the context of empowerment, employee's self-efficacy beliefs has been assessed as the measure of psychological empowerment. Hence, the present work focuses on two dimensions viz., participative decision-making and self-efficacy to measure the level of employee empowerment.

Elements of Employee Empowerment

(i) **Participative Decision Making:** Participation in decision-making (PDM), defined as sharing decision making with others to achieve organizational objectives, is found as a managerial practice that increases subordinate initiative and contributions to the processes of decision making. PDM aims to increase the participation of employees by providing them with greater discretion, attention, influence, support, information, and other resources; and to share the issue of problem solving with followers by consulting them before making a decision (Bass, 1990). It has been consistently found to be an effective managerial approach to accomplish structural empowerment (Chisholm & Vansina, 1993). Nonaka (1988) pointed out that the sharing of information freely across levels and functions is a critical ingredient for individual autonomy. Randolph (2000) has argued that when managers share vital information with their employees in an effort to empower them, then employees will feel a sense of trust, which enhances their willingness to use their knowledge, experience, and motivation in the pursuit of organizational goals. Similarly, Block (1987) contended that to create an empowering environment, managers should ensure that information cascades throughout an organization. Previous literature suggests that through participation in decision making, employees gain a sense of ownership and authority of their work which ultimately lead to increase in their attitudes and behaviours such as employee motivation, job satisfaction, organizational commitment and organizational citizenship behaviour (e.g., Scott-Ladd & Chan, 2004; Pearson & Duffy, 1999; Van Yperen, van den Berg, & Willering 1999).

(ii) **Self-Efficacy:** It is defined as, 'the conviction that one can successfully execute the behavior required to produce the outcomes' (Bandura, 1977). Self-efficacy can be influenced by the direct experience of mastering a task, by observing others' successful performance, or through praise and encouragement expressed by a superior (Bandura 1986). Conger and Kanungo (1988) suggested that in order to be cognitively consistent with a new role of enlarged responsibility and authority, empowered employees would have the self-image that they are efficacious and are responsible for service outcomes. This indicates that along with the structural component (participation in decision making), there are certain psychological mechanisms which are responsible for making the employees feel 'empowered'. Occupational self-efficacy has been defined as the belief in ability and competence to perform in an occupation (Pethe, Chaudhari, & Dhar, 1999). Self-efficacy beliefs are necessary for individuals to believe that their self-determined actions will yield the desired results. The results of increased self-efficacy beliefs are increased amounts of effort by individuals, because they believe they can put forth the effort required to master the level of performance desired by the organization (Fulford & Enz, 1995).

CHAPTER 6

Employee Training

Investing in developmental HR practices implies providing employees with new knowledge, skills and abilities, thus, offering them the opportunity to develop and in turn, perform more effectively. Continuous training and professional development is not a luxury but a necessity of today's changing economy as in order to cope with the changing business environment and to exploit the future job opportunities training programmes are very useful to make the employees up to date and industry ready. Employee training is at the heart of modern management practice in any organization. Therefore, development of high potential workers with the support of the continuous training and retraining is seen as a core element in the development of the competitive advantage of the organizations.

Definition

Employee training as one of the most widespread human resources (HR) practices refers to systematic activities to develop and improve employees' skills, knowledge and behaviours to enable them to perform job-related duties, accomplish specific tasks and meet the quality requirements of HR for the future.

Theoretical Framework

Evaluation of training effectiveness is a system for measuring changes due to training interventions—most important, whether trainees have achieved learning outcomes (Goldstein & Ford, 2002; Kraiger, McLinden & Casper, 199). In the bottom line business world of today, the concerned professionals should place a very high priority on evaluation of training, but in most cases, it just hasn't happened (Ford, 2000). The primary function of evaluation for training is to enhance a trainee's knowledge, skills, and ability to improve his or her performance. Previous research on training evaluation has called for the use of multidimensional criteria in assessing training effectiveness (Campbell, McCloy, Oppler & Sager, 1993; Kraiger *et al.*, 1993). According to Saxena (2011), the training effectiveness can be best evaluated on the basis of overall training process and not the training outcomes. According to Kirkpatrick's (1959, 1960) classic and very popular hierarchical model of training outcomes, there are four main levels at which training can be evaluated. These are in terms of participants' immediate reaction to the training itself (level 1 – reaction), what they learned from the training (level 2 – learning), the extent to which the new learning is transferred back to the job and results in new forms of behaviour at work (level 3 – behaviour), and the extent to which the new job behaviours result in improved individual and organizational performance (level 4 – results). According to the Sugrue and Rivera (2005), the results of the industry report revealed that training evaluations occurred at the following rates: level one (employee reaction) 91%; level two (employee knowledge) 54%; level three (transfer of training to the workplace) 23%; level four (impact on business) 8%; and level five (monetary impact of the training) 3%. This research indicates that the primary means by which organizations evaluate training programs are trainee reactions, or the subjective evaluations learners make about their training experiences (Sitzmann *et al.*, 2008). Such reactions are trainee's response to training activities, which is based on his/her opinions, observations, judgments, perceptions, and understanding about the training programme as well as his/her performance (Rajeev *et al.*, 2009). Oostrom and van Mierlo (2008) clearly specified that this response is post-training. This level of evaluation focuses on the key stakeholder, i.e., the trainee who responds only by showing his/her behavior towards training, and therefore, researchers prefer the aspects of authenticity and usefulness of measuring trainees' reactions so that accuracy is ensured (Kirkpatrick & Kirkpatrick, 2006). Literature on comparative HRM has called for more direct comparisons of HRM practices in different countries in order to understand the variety of practices within different contexts (Hendry, 1991; Easterby-Smith, Malina, & Yu, 1995). This provides some of the motivation for the research to evaluate the practice of employee training which is perceived as the most important HR practice (Jennings, Cyr & Moore, 1995). In the present study, it is intended to assess the effectiveness of employee training practice in the selected banks by investigating the design and implementation of training system in the selected banks and the extent to which such training is provided to the employees.

Elements of Employee Training

(i) **Commitment to training participation:** Successful training requires commitment and employees who expect benefits from their participation in training activities are more committed to their organizations and so be more willing to participate in an organization's training activities (Bulut & Culha, 2010; Ahmad & Bakar ,2003; Bartlett, 2001; Newman, Thanacoody & Hui, 2011). If employees feel that their training would be beneficial for both themselves and the organization, and there would be chances to use and practice what was gained from the training, their degree of willingness to participate in future organizational training, and the outcomes from training, are likely to be greater (Facteau *et al.*, 1995).

(ii) **Access to training opportunities:** It is the extent to which employees feel that sufficient training opportunities are made available to them by the organization and their supervisors or managers. Training opportunities may, therefore, serve a general purpose in making the employees feel important and taken care of, in terms of having opportunities to develop. Providing the training and development opportunities to employees not only enhances the knowledge and skills of employee but also effect on the behavior of employee (Pajo, Coetzer & Guenole, 2010). Firms with higher levels of perceived fair access to organizational training programmes will be more likely to increase the number of committed employees in their organization (Bartlett & Kang, 2004; Newman, Thanacoody & Hui, 2011) leading to superior organizational performance (Guest, 1997; Purcell, 1999). When employees perceive that there is access to training, they feel their organizations have been willing to invest in them and care about them. In turn, employees tend to work harder, attach themselves to their organizations and display organizational citizenship (Bulut & Culha, 2010). At the same time, an equitable and open approach to the access to organizational training increases both the trainees' and all other organization members' commitment to their organizations (Podsakoff, MacKenzie, Paine & Bachrach, 2000).

(iii) **Relevance of training:** Relevance of training implies that training opportunities provided to the employees are relevant to their current and future role. Employees expect that training opportunities should allow promotions and improvements in their current role and development of skills for future job role. No organization can get a candidate who exactly matches with the job and organizational requirement, hence, relevant training is important to develop the employee and make him/ her suitable to the job. Thus, it is imperative to determine whether the training opportunities provided by an organization are relevant to an employee's current and future job role.

(iv) **Usefulness or benefits of training:** Trainee reactions are also importantly influenced by the perceived usefulness of the training (Warr & Bunce, 1995; Warr, Allan & Birdi, 1999). Giangreco *et al.* (2009)

found that that the perceived usefulness of training is the strongest predictor of training satisfaction. Noe & Wilk (1993) suggested that training leads to personal benefits i.e., the extent to which employees believe that participation in training activities help them in improving their job performance and making progress towards their personal development. The values added from training and development as perceived by the employees will be increased task performance (Dysvik & Kuwaas, 2008) and improved employee performance (Kraiger *et al.*, 2004). Thus, it is important to determine whether the program has a positive effect on job performance and, if so, how great it is (Buckley & Caple, 2000; Guthrie & Schwoerer, 1996).

(v) **Satisfaction with training:** Satisfaction with the training is one of commonly measured reaction and evaluates how well trainees like the training programme using data on their perceptions, satisfaction with programme objectives, content, instruction, delivery, and trainers (Tian, Atkinson, Portnoy & Gold, 2007).

CHAPTER 7

Quality of Work Life

Organizational Justice

Quality of work life (QWL) is a comprehensive construct that includes an individual's job related well-being and the extent to which work experiences are rewarding, fulfilling and devoid of stress and other negative personal consequences (Shamir & Saloman, 1985). Saklani (2004) defined QWL as the existence of a 'work environment' which is a matter of certain humanistic and life-enhancing work experience characteristics, as perceived by people in the organizations. Certain working conditions and management practices such as, reasonable pay, healthy physical environment, employees' welfare, job security, equal treatment in job related matters, grievance handling, opportunity to grow and develop, good human relations, participation in decision making and balance in life are some of the key components of this humanistic and life-enhancing 'work environment'. Fundamentally, quality of work life builds on the concept that employees have the potential of making valuable contribution to ensure organizational success. Therefore, employees should be treated with fairness, respect and dignity at workplaces. Improvement in QWL is considered necessary not only because it contributes to organizational efficiency and to a fall in negative employee behaviour but also because justice and fair play demand it (Chan & Wyatt, 2007).

Definition

Organizational Justice (OJ) deals with the role of fairness as a consideration in the workplace or more specifically, with employee's perceptions of fairness in their employment relationship. The principles of justice, fair and equity should be taken care of in disciplinary procedure, grievance procedures, promotions, transfers, demotion, work assignment, leave, etc., in order to ensure better QWL.

Theoretical Framework

In a study of Indian organizations, Saklani (2004) found equity and justice among other factors, as important components of QWL. Employees experience decision-making in their day to day work life and they judge those decisions, their outcomes as well as the way such decisions are communicated to them by asking themselves, 'Am I being treated fairly'? These subjective perceptions about justice as fairness in organizations have been one of the most active research areas in the behavioural science for last four decades. Sheppard, Lewicki and Minton (1992) presented two principles to judge the justice of a decision, procedure, or action. The first principle of justice requires a judgment of balance. This principle requires one to compare a given decision against other similar decisions in similar situations. Comparisons of balance are made by evaluating the outcomes of two or more people and equating those outcomes to the value of the inputs they provide to the organization. The second principle by which a decision, procedure, or action is evaluated is correctness. This can be considered as the quality which makes the decision seem right. Therefore, one makes decisions about the perceived justice of some action that harms or benefits someone by deciding whether the action appears to be both balanced as well as correct. Organizational justice (OJ) refers to the extent to which employee perceives workplace procedures, outcomes and interactions to be fair in nature. A high level of perceived equity signals to employees that the organization supports them and has their well-being at heart (Eisenberger, Huntington, Hutchison & Sowa, 1986).

Employees are considered as the pivotal factor of any service-oriented organization like banking, and play a significant role in improving its effectiveness. Organizational justice has been considered as a critical practice to create a positive work environment and foster a sense of organizational concern and support among employees. Earlier research on OJ in Indian and other cultural contexts has focused on the unique effects of justice dimensions on key outcomes such as job satisfactions, organizational commitment, organizational citizenship behavior, turnover intentions, etc. Further, a fuller understanding of the fairness judgment requires a simultaneous examination of the three dimensions (distributive, procedural and interactional justice) which is found scarce in the literature as most of the studies focused on either one or two dimensions of OJ. Totawar and Nambudiri (2011) in their empirical study of 139 managers from public sector units in India found that organizational justice positively influence job satisfaction and quality of work life mediates this relationship. In their empirical study of 300 Malaysian managers and non-managers, Fatt, Khin and Heng (2010) found that higher level of distributive and procedural justice perceptions increases the level of employees' job satisfaction and organizational commitment while reduces turnover intention. The study of Nadiri and Tanova (2010) showed that the perceptions of organizational justice have a strong effect on organizational citizenship behavior and job satisfaction. Bakshi, Kumar and Rani (2009) explored the relationship between perceived organizational justice, job satisfaction and organization commitment and found that distributive justice was significantly related to job satisfaction whereas procedural justice was not found to be related significantly with job satisfaction; however, distributive justice was found significantly related to job satisfaction whereas procedural justice was not found to be related significantly with job satisfaction. These studies clearly showed that organizational justice is a significant mechanism or practice that strongly influences various individual attitudes and behaviours. Earlier researchers have observed a clear diversity in the ways of conceptualizing justice from the focus on process control (Thibaut & Walker, 1975), shifting to consistency (Leventhal, 1980) and then on interpersonal treatment (Bies & Moag, 1986). Subsequent researchers emphasized the distribution of payment and other work-related rewards derived from equity theory (Greenberg, 1987). However, this outcome based perspective ignored the procedures or means through which such outcomes are received. Therefore, most of the research about organizational justice has then focused on two major issues: firstly, employees' responses to the outcomes they receive, that is, the distributive justice and, secondly, the means or procedures by which they obtain these outcomes, that is, the procedural justice (Cropanzano & Greenberg, 1997). A few studies provide evidence that people consider the nature of their treatment by others also as a determinant of fairness (e.g., Bies, 1986; Tyler, 1988). Thus, the quality of the interpersonal treatment received was also considered as a major determinant of people's assessment of fair treatment (Greenberg, 1990). Interactional (interpersonal) justice may be sought by showing concern for individuals regarding the distributive outcomes they received (Greenberg, 1993). Although few researchers have treated interactional justice as a component of procedural justice (e.g., Moorman, 1991; Niehoff & Moorman, 1993; Tyler & Bies, 1990), many others have considered it independently as a third type of justice (e.g., Aquino, 1995; Barling & Phillips, 1993; Bies & Shapiro, 1987; Skarlicki & Folger, 1997). Colquitt (2001) empirically tested the dimensionality of organizational justice and suggested a three-dimension structure of OJ as procedural justice, distributive justice and interactional justice. Following Colquit's suggestion, it may be argued that all the three components are equally significant as an organization that encourages distributive, procedural and interactional justice in toto, benefits both, the employee as well as the organization; employees will be satisfied that they have been treated fairly and the organization will be benefitted by positive attitudes and behaviours of those satisfied employees. They can be meaningfully treated as three components of overall fairness (Ambrose & Arnaud, 2005; Ambrose & Schminke, 2007), and the three components can work together.

Elements of Organizational Justice

(i) **Distributive justice:** it refers to the fairness of decision outcomes. Most researches on distributive justice have focused on the equity rule. Leventhal (1976) described the equity rule as a single normal rule which dictates that reward and resources be distributed in accordance with recipients' contributions.

(ii) **Procedural justice:** it is referred as the fairness of procedures leading to a particular outcome. Procedural justice can outweigh distributive justice i.e, people may be willing to accept an unwanted outcome if they believe that decision leading to that outcome was conducted according to organizational justice principles. For example, Greenberg (1994) found that smokers easily accepted a smoking ban at their workplace when they felt that they had been given thorough information about the changes of policy, in a socially sensitive manner. Procedural justice can be ensured if complete and accurate information is collected to take any decision regarding the employees or when promotion decisions are based on employee performance rather than favouritism or if employees are allowed to challenge or appeal against ill-advised decisions.

(iii) **Interactional justice:** it refers to the quality of interpersonal treatment received by employees particularly as part of formal decision making procedures. Colquitt (2001) has conceptually and empirically showed that interactional justice constitutes two components which are informational justice (related to explanations and social accounts) and interpersonal justice (related to respectful consideration and sensitivity). Thus, interactional justice is fostered when decision makers treat employees with respect and sensitivity and explain the rationale for decisions thoroughly. Skarlicki and Latham (1997) in an experimental study trained union leaders to behave more justly and they were taught to provide explanations and apologies (informational justice) and to treat their reports with courtesy and respect (interpersonal justice). It was observed that after three months, individuals who reported to trained leaders exhibited more helpful citizenship behaviors as compared to individuals who reported to untrained leaders.

CHAPTER

8

Quality of Work Life

Work-Life Balance

Work and life are two interlinked components of an employee and any positive or negative experience in one component creates a similar impact in other component. If employees are stressed out at work, the stress can spill over to their personal life affecting the way they view work and life, which could disrupt work-life balance. Personal and family responsibility is neglected in the process of securing an economic prospect; hence, it deteriorates the interaction of family life that reduces QWL. The ultimate goal of HRD in any country is to improve the quality of life of all its people and not merely concerned with providing necessary skills to individuals (Bacchus, 1992). As the work and family are the most crucial domains in most people's lives, therefore, balancing these two domains is essential for the well-being of the individual (Fisher, Bulger & Smith, 2009). The growing emphasis on achievement of work-life balance among today's professionals has led the organizations to understand that how any perceived 'imbalance' or conflict between work and family arises and by what means it might be alleviated if they are to motivate and retain their talented employees.

Definition

Work-life balance has been defined as 'satisfaction and good functioning at work and at home with a minimum of role conflict' (Clark, 2000) or in simpler terms, it is the balance of an individual's levels of work and private life. Thus, organizations implement work-life benefits programs and policies to help employees with the many facets of their lives including their personal well-being, professional development, and family responsibilities (McShane & Von Glinow, 2000).

Theoretical Framework

Family-friendly firms have a significant impact on the lives and careers of business professionals who work in them (Friedman & Greenhaus, 2000). Consequently, organizations are equally concerned to reduce the employee stress and thus acknowledge the importance of the work-life balance programmes and policies to attract and maintain highly skilled employees (Joshi *et al.*, 2002) by introducing and providing work-life balance policies such as flexible work hours, childcare programmes, flexible leave, reducing work hours, part-time jobs, compressed working time for their employees (Liddicoat, 2003). The perceptions of work-life balance will benefit organizational outcomes such as actual turnover through positive employee attitudes (Simons & Roberson, 2003). WLB perceptions are also found to positively correlated to individual outcomes such as job satisfaction (Kanwar, Singh & Kodwani, 2009). Kossek and Ozeki (1998) suggest that employers need to develop creative ways to redesign the workplace to allow employees to better meet varying family demands. These findings provide a strong basis for implementing family friendly work–family balance programmes in organizations. Since jobs in banking sector were believed to be comfortable enough to maintain a good work life balance, past research work has not adequately addressed the influence of work-life balance with respect to banking employees. But with the ever growing competition in this segment and influx of private and foreign banks, the work-life balance component of quality of work life cannot be ignored. This study therefore extends the work-life balance literature by assessing the WLB of employees in banking sector and how this may influence their attitude in terms of citizenship behaviour. In this study we have replaced the policy and programme related concept of work–life balance by combining three factors namely, work-family spillover, work-family conflict and work-family facilitation, to arrive at a more complete picture of the determinants of work-life balance. This was necessary to present a more focused indicator of work–life balance which captured the spillover, conflict and satisfaction effects of work place on the employees' domestic life.

Elements of Work-life Balance

Work-family spillover: It emphasize the consequences of the work for family relations and it seeks to capture the effects of work on time for partner/family as well as time for family responsibilities and personal pursuits (Maume & Houston, 2001). It has been shown that actual hours worked is the largest influence on work-family spillover (White *et al.*, 2003).

Work–family conflict: A lack of balance between work and non-work is commonly conceptualized as work/family conflict or work/non-work conflict (e.g., Frone *et al.*, 1997; Parasuraman *et al.*, 1996). It can happen both when work roles interfere with non-work roles and vice versa. The focus here is on the former relationship, as it considers work/life balance in the context of the impact of work on non-work or family role. Kossek and Ozeki (1998, 1999) found that while most HR policy research is designed with the assumption that the use of organizational policies to support family roles will reduce work-family conflict, relatively few studies on HR policies actually measures work-family conflict. It has been shown that the number of hours worked have an important influence on the degree of conflict that may be experienced and contributes directly to feelings of work/non-work conflict (e.g., Sturges & Guest, 2004; Frone *et al.*, 1997; Parasuraman *et al.*, 1996).

Work–family facilitation: An empirical study carried out by van Steenbergen and Ellemers (2009) shows that employees who experience low conflict and high facilitation between work and family roles are objectively healthier, less absent and better performing employees. Carlson and Perrewe (1999) have demonstrated that a supportive culture at work can reduce the degree of work/family conflict individuals experience and enhance the perception that an organization 'cares' about its employees (Lambert, 2000).

CHAPTER 9

Fundamentals of Organizational Citizenship Behaviour

Introduction

Organization Citizenship Behaviour (OCB) has emerged as an exciting field of research more than two decades ago when Organ (1988) proposed that organizational citizenship behavior could influence individual and organization performance and since then OCB has become one of the extensively researched construct in the organizational behavior literature. According to Vigoda-Gadot (2007), almost 300 studies have examined this phenomenon and emphasized its importance to management studies across sectors and cultures; concluding that these spontaneous behaviors by individuals have played a key role in increasing the effectiveness, efficiency, and positive climate in the workplace. OCB has therefore been identified as an important indicator of employees' performance that goes beyond formal duties and has a major positive impact on organizational outcomes, service quality, effectiveness, and long-range sustainability.

Definition of OCB

It is defined as, "OCB represents individual behavior that is discretionary, not directly or explicitly recognized by the formal reward system, and that in the aggregate promotes the effective functioning of the organization" (Bateman & Organ, 1983; Smith, Organ, & Near, 1983). Organ further explained, "By discretionary, we mean that the behavior is not an enforceable requirement of the role or the job description, that is, the clearly specifiable terms of the person's employment contract with the organization; the behavior is rather a matter of personal choice, such that its omission is not generally understood as punishable. Examples of these efforts include cooperation with peers, performing extra duties without complaint, punctuality, volunteering and helping others, using time efficiently, conserving resources, sharing ideas and positively representing the organization (Turnipseed & Rassuli, 2005). To make it more specific, Organ (1997) refined his definition, conceptualizing organizational citizenship behavior as, "performance that supports the social or psychological environment in which the task performance takes place-"a definition that more closely corresponds to contextual performance, as proposed by Borman and Motowidlo (1993). Further definitions of OCB were given by other researchers as well, e.g., Lee and Allen (2002) defined OCB as "employee behaviors that, although not critical to the task or job, serve to facilitate organizational functioning". Then, Lambert (2006) described OCB as "behavior that (a) goes beyond the basic requirements of the job, (b) is to a large extent discretionary, and (c) is of benefit to the organization". Despite a number of definitions and redefinitions of this construct, there is a consensus in this particular field that OCB addresses silent behaviours for organizational enterprises (Barbuto, Brown, Wilhite, & Wheeler, 2001). Vigoda-Gadot (2007) claimed that a common denominator of the most of the OCB studies is that, for the most part, they have treated OCB as a constructive, self-initiated, spontaneous, or voluntary behavior aimed at enhancing the productivity of the workplace.

History of OCB

The concept of organization citizenship behaviour has its roots in 1930s when Chester Barnard observed "extra role behaviors" demonstrated by the employees (Barnard 1938). Barnard (1938) stated that the willingness of individuals to contribute cooperative efforts to the organization was indispensable to effective attainment of organizational goals. He further explained that efforts must be exerted not only to perform the functions that contribute to the goals of the organization, but also to maintain the organization itself. Later, Katz and Kahn, (1966) defined "supra-role behaviors" that improved the effectiveness of the organization and explained them as those behaviors that, "includes any gestures that lubricate the social machinery of the organization and do not directly adhere to the usual notion of task performance". Katz and Kahn coined the term "citizenship" to represent the workers that displayed these extra-role behaviors.

Dimensions of OCB

Researchers hold different views with respect to the dimensionality of OCB. A review of the literature reports over 30 dimensions of OCBs, with considerable variation in the nature of behaviours (Podsakoff *et al.*, 2000). Smith *et al.* (1983) described OCB as having two basic dimensions: altruism and generalized compliance. In his attempt to further define organizational citizenship behavior, Organ (1988) highlights five specific categories of discretionary behavior. The five dimensions identified by Organ are altruism (welfare), courtesy, conscientiousness (compliance), sportsmanship and civic virtue. Altruism: helping of an individual co-worker on a task; courtesy: alerting others in the organization about changes that may affect their work; conscientiousness: carrying out one's duties beyond the minimum requirements; sportsmanship: refraining from complaining about trivial matters; and civic virtue: participating in the governance of the organization. Williams and Anderson (1991) proposed a two-dimensional conceptualization of OCB on the basis of Organ's (1988) five-dimension taxonomy: OCB-I (behaviours directed toward individuals, compromising altruism and courtesy) and OCB-O (behaviours directed toward the organization, comprising the remaining three-dimension in Organ's (1988) conceptualization). Podsakoff and Mackenzie (1994) modified the categorizations, merged altruism and courtesy and termed it 'helping'. Empirical research on the dimensions of organizational citizenship behaviors (OCB) has generated somewhat conflicting results. Few researchers have been successful in identifying four categories of OCB (Moorman & Blakely, 1995), but the weight of the factor analytic evidence suggested a two-factor structure. Skarlicki and Latham (1995) examined OCB in a university setting and their data also supported a two-factor structure,. organizational and interpersonal. Farh, Earley & Lin (1997) found two other emic dimensions (Interpersonal Harmony and Protecting Company Resources). Deckop, Mangel and Cirka (1999) have utilized a uni-dimensional or overall OCB measure in their research. Podsakoff *et al.*, (2000) presented seven common themes or dimensions on OCB: Helping Behavior, Sportsmanship, Organizational Loyalty, Organizational Compliance, Individual Initiative, Civic Virtue, and Self Development. In two separate factor analytic studies, DiPaola and Tschannen-Moran (2001) found that there are not five separate dimensions of the construct, or even two for that matter, but rather that one dimension captures all aspects of OCB. According to them, both, benefits to the organization (helping the organization) and benefits to the individual (helping individuals) combine into a single, bipolar construct. As cited by Bogler & Somech (2004), researches suggested other dimensions such as, various types of participation (Van Dyne, Graham & Dienesch, 1994); and helping and voice (Stamper & Van Dyne, 2001; Van Dyne & LePine, 1998). The most widely studied forms of this behaviour include altruism and courtesy (Organ, 1988), helping and cooperating with others (Borman & Motowidlo, 1993; Podsakoff & MacKenzie, 1994), and interpersonal facilitation (Van Scotter & Motowidlo, 1996). However, 'helping' behaviours have been described by Podsakoff *et al.* (2000) as being an important form of citizenship behaviour by 'virtually everyone who has worked in this area'. Walz and Niehoff (1996) examined how OCB explained a variety of performance measures in limited-menu restaurants and they found that the combination of helping behaviour, sportsmanship and civic virtue accounted for an average of about 28% of the variance of six objective performance measures (including financial results and customer satisfaction). Borman, Penner, Allen & Motowidlo (2001) finds Altruism and conscientiousness are the two major or overarching dimensions of OCB. A recent meta-analysis conducted by Hoffman, Blair, Meriac & Woehr (2007) suggested that the current operationalization of OCB is best viewed as indicator of a general OCB factor and there is likely little to be gained through the use of separate dimensional measures as opposed to an overall composite measure. A similar conclusion was reached by a previous meta-analysis (LePine, Erez, & Johnson, 2002). A meta-analysis by Podsakoff, MacKenzie, Paine & Bachrach (2000) showed that helping behavior increases moral cohesiveness and belonging sense of a team which results into high performance and low turnover inside the organization. Chaitanya and Tripathi (2001) found that helping (altruism) is based on loyalty of the employee towards the organization i.e., employees who are really loyal to the organization will have a helping (altruistic) inclination. Yoon and Suh (2003) in a study of Korean travel agencies found that contact employees' sportsmanship related positively and significantly with customer service quality as perceived by customers. According to Turnipseed and Rassuli (2005), OCB elements which enhance performance include: elements which add social capital, helping or altruistic elements, elements resulting with time savings or problem solving and other elements which provide socio-emotional support by boosting morale or developing a nurturing culture.

When employees behave as good organizational citizens toward each other, they promote a positive internal climate, which in turn may have a positive impact in the way customers are served and lead these to form positive images of the organization (Chien, 2004). Over the period, helping behaviour may work as a 'disseminating mechanism' through which 'best practices' are spread throughout the organizations. When people help each other, managers remain free to focus on more productive activities (Rego & Cunha, 2008). Helping, courteous and sportsmanship behaviours promote a positive climate within the branch or organization, inducing higher creativity and performance (Wright & Cropanzano, 2004). Rego and Cunha (2008) asserted that sportsmanship, courtesy, helping and interpersonal harmony creates a positive climate among employees that spills over to customers. They further stated that high levels of helping, courtesy and sportsmanship build esprit de corps among co-workers, thus promoting employee cooperation for facing problems with customers and for tackling challenges and opportunities. Furthermore, employees who help customers and behave courteously towards them may foster the sense of gratitude in customers, leading them to repeat the service acquisition, to disseminate a positive image of the organization (thus attracting more customers) and to be loyal even when the 'appeals' of competitors are 'seductive'. Following Rego and Cunha's suggestions it can be said that the three dimensions of OCB viz., helping behavior, courtesy and sportsmanship, in the aggregate, may facilitate a more positive and effective organizational climate among employees and between them and their supervisors, ultimately improving customer services leading to better organizational performance. Hence, the present text employed a three-dimensional approach to analyze OCB, rather than the traditional five-dimensional approach.

(i) **Helping behaviour** or altruism is defined as, voluntary actions that help another coworker with a work problem – instructing a new hire on how to use equipment, helping a coworker catch up with a backlog of work, fetching materials that a colleague needs and cannot procure on his own (Organ, 1988). Conceptually in the present work, helping behavior involves voluntarily helping others with, or preventing the occurrence of, work related problems, help training new employees, helping customers even when this is not part of their job or even if they visit after working hours and producing highest quality customer services regardless of circumstances.

(ii) **Courtesy** is defined as, all of those foresightful gestures that help someone else prevent a problem - 'touching base' with people before committing to actions that will affect them, providing advanced notice to someone who needs to know to schedule work. The concept of courtesy in present research measures behaviours such as taking steps to try to prevent conflicts with co-workers, boosting up others when they are stressed by work related problems, always willing to listen to co-worker problems, willingly share expertise with other co-workers, treating customers with respect, speaking courteously with every customer (that is, regardless of their social or economic status).

(iii) **Sportsmanship** is defined as a willingness to tolerate the inevitable inconveniences and impositions of work without complaining (Organ, 1990). Further, Podsakoff, Mackenzie, Paine & Bachrach (2000) opinionated that "good sports" are people who not only do not complain when they are inconvenienced by others, but also maintain a positive attitude even when things do not go their way, are not offended when others do not follow their suggestions, are willing to sacrifice their personal interest for the good of the work group, and do not take the rejection of their ideas personally. This dimension in the present work considers employee behaviours such as refraining from consuming a lot of time complaining about trivial matters, not to pass difficult or unpleasant task to others, voluntarily attempting to improve competence, trying to solve problems on their own before presenting them to the superior manager, avoiding taking extra responsibilities at work and volunteering for overtime work when it is required.

CHAPTER

10

An Integrated Model of HRD and Organizational Citizenship Behaviour

Introduction

Human resource development (HRD) is increasingly gaining recognition as a key practice in maximizing the internal capabilities of the firm, and thus enhancing its capacity to compete. There is a growing consensus among researchers and academicians that individual employee performance has implications on organizational level outcomes and collective performance of human resources in an organization provides it a unique source of competitive advantage that is difficult to imitate. Dyer & Reeves (1995) suggested that there are four types of outcomes which might apply to research pertaining to human resource strategy. These include: employee related outcomes, (2) organizational outcomes, (3) financial outcomes, and (4) market outcomes. They emphasized that human resource strategies will have their most direct effects on employee related outcomes, followed by organizational outcomes, and so on. Similarly, Becker, Huselid, Pinckus & Spratt (1997) suggested that HR practices influence the behaviours of employees which then affect operational, financial, and share price outcomes. These two views suggested that a thorough understanding of the relationships between HR practices and employee outcomes is critical to our ability to draw logical inferences concerning the HR-performance causal chain as a whole. Besides, there have been calls to focus more on employee-centred outcomes and not only on the effects of HRM on organizational performance (Boxall & Macky 2009; Guest 1997; Nishii & Wright 2008). Consequently, there is a need to understand the employee related outcomes or mechanisms that underlie this relationship between HR practices and organizational performance.

HRD and OCB

A summary of earlier studies on HRD climate, practices and organizational outcomes presented in Exhibit 10.1 indicates that human resources are the most valuable assets and their development and wellbeing is necessary to achieve competitive advantage in a global market. It is also evident that the employee attitudes and behaviours still remain very important variables to examine in organizations because of their inherent nature to influence the overall efficiency and profitability of organizations. Extant literature in this field confirmed that HR practices have significant effect on organizational performance outcomes such as productivity, job satisfaction, turnover intentions, employee engagement, organizational commitment and organizational citizenship behaviour. The sum of the earlier research works clearly reflects that a number of studies have been carried out by previous researchers on various aspects of HRD sub-systems and organizational citizenship behaviours (OCB) such as their assessment, antecedents, consequences, impact, relationships, etc. Previous researches contributed significantly to HRD and OCB literature. While a number of previous research studies have focused on specific HRD sub-systems either in isolation or in combination, none of them addressed the development focussed bundles of practices like performance appraisal, employee training, employee empowerment, organizational justice and work-life balance alongwith general HRD climate in an integrated form.

Proposed Conceptual Framework

The integration of various HRD practices implemented by the organizations such as performance appraisal, training, career development, potential appraisal, counseling and feedback, rewards and recognition, quality of work life, succession planning, empowerment and communication, etc. helps to create an environment which is conducive for the development of employee competencies and their well-being and in exchange employees are willing to 'go to that extra mile' and make significant and visible contribution to the organization's performance. A growing body of literature reveals that substantial investment in human capital and the implementation of human resource management (HRM) practices may enhance corporate financial performance (Huselid, 1995; Huselid, Jackson & Schuler, 1997; Vandenberg, Richardson, & Eastman, 1999) and signal to employees that they represent a major source of competitive advantage for the company (Fiorito, Bozeman & Young, 1997) leading in turn to a greater sense of organizational attachment. More specifically, research reviewed by Shore, Tetrick, Lynch and Barksdale (2006) clearly suggests that higher levels of organizational investment are associated with social exchange relationships that create feelings of employee obligation which in turn influences employees to benefit the organization through behaviors that exceed minimal requirements of employment.

Exhibit 10.1: A Summary of Review of Earlier Studies

Author (s)/ Researcher(s) and Year	Study Variable(s): Independent variables	Study Variable(s): Dependent variables	Key Findings of the Study
(1)	(2)	(3)	(4)
Priyadarshini and Venkatapathy (2003)	HRD practices	Organizational effectiveness (OE)	Private sector banks have weaker HRD practices as compared to nationalized banks. Positive impact of HRDP on OE.
Ahmad and Bakar (2003)	Training	Organizational commitment	Availability of training, support for training, motivation to learn, training environment, perceived benefits of training were all significantly correlated with overall organizational commitment.
Rainaye (2004)	Training policy and practice	–	Line managers were not found to be well involved in employee development; induction training was not found in sufficient duration, evaluation of training was not found proper, and senior executives were not found to have proper interaction with subordinate employees.
Jain and Kamble (2005)	Performance appraisal	–	Most of the PAS design/ content variables, process variables and outcome variables were found to be highly and positively correlated to the overall effectiveness of PAS.

(Contd…)

(1)	(2)	(3)	(4)
Bhatnagar and Sandhu (2005)	Psychological empowerment	Organizational citizenship behaviour.	Psychological empowerment (meaning, Impact and self-determination) is strongly related to Organizational citizenship behaviour.
Moideenkutty, Blau & Nalakanth (2005)	Managerial evaluations of employee performance	Objective productivity & OCB	Both objective productivity and OCB are significantly related to subjective performance evaluations.
Purang (2006)	HRD climate	–	Better HRD climate in private & multinationals as compared to public sector.
Jawahar (2006)	Satisfaction with performance appraisal feedback	Job Satisfaction, Organizational commitment, Turnover Intention	Satisfaction with appraisal feedback was positively related to job satisfaction and organizational commitment and negatively related to turnover intentions.
Pare and Tremblay (2007)	HR practices (HRP)	Procedural Justice(PJ), Organizational commitment (OC,) Citizenship behaviour (OCB), Turnover intention(TI)	HR practices, OCB and OC are negatively & significantly related to TI. HRP is positively and significantly related to OCB. PJ mediates the relationship between HRP & OCB and TI.
Gupta (2007)	Employee Empowerment (Empowering factors and consequences)	–	Open communication and Organizational commitment was ranked highest and low formalization and self-efficacy was ranked lowest.
Rao, Rao and Yadav (2007)	HRD subsystems	–	Performance management system, and training and development system are most matured systems. Organization Development and feedback and counseling are in the next level of maturity. Potential appraisal and career planning and development are the least developed and used subsystems.

(Contd…)

(1)	(2)	(3)	(4)
Sun, Aryee, and Law (2007)	High performance HR practices (HRP)	OCB, Turnover Intentions (TI), Productivity	Positive relationship between HRP and OCB and Productivity. Negative relationship between HRP & TI. OCB mediates the relationship between HRP & TI & Productivity.
Jain and Agrawal (2007)	Training system and process, HRD climate		Trainees' satisfaction level in public sector institutes was perceived higher as compared to the private sector institutes. HRD climate was found as moderately favourable.
Gupta (2007)	Empowerment factors & empowerment consequences		All the variables in public sector unit scored higher than the scores of the variables of R&D unit except for Self efficacy.
Dysvik and Kuvaas (2008)	Perceived training opportunities (PTO)	Intrinsic motivation, Task performance (TP) OCB, Turnover intentions (TI)	Relationship between PTO, and both TP and OCB were fully mediated, and that the relationship between PTO and TI was partially mediated by employee intrinsic motivation.
Purang (2008)	HRD climate	Organizational commitment	Positive relationship between the variables
Jha and Nair (2008)	Internal locus of control, job characteristics, and superior-subordinate relationship	Psychological empowerment	All the three variables positively influence the psychological empowerment.
Saxena and Tiwari (2009)	HRD climate	–	Average HRD climate was found

(Contd…)

(1)	(2)	(3)	(4)
Buddhapriya (2009)	Work-life support		Commitment to family responsibility' and 'lack of gender sensitive policies by the employer' are considered as important barriers which affect the career advancement of women professionals to senior positions. Strong provisions for factors like flexible working hours, childcare facilitates and emergency care for children and elders support for non-work commitment, wellness, personal development programmes and flexibility in work location were required to achieve better work-life balance.
Kanwar, Singh and Kodwani (2009)	Work life balance and burnout	Job satisfaction	Work-life balance and job satisfaction were positively related to each other. De-motivation, exhaustion and meaninglessness were negatively related to job satisfaction.
Dickinson (2009)	Job satisfaction, relationship with supervisor, fairness perceptions, organizational commitment, job stress, and outside the workplace.	Organizational citizenship behavior	A positive relationship between relationship with supervisor, organizational commitment, job stress, and organizational citizenship behavior. No significant relationship was found between job satisfaction, fairness perceptions, stress outside the workplace, and organizational citizenship behavior.
Wei, Han and Hsu (2010)	HR Practices (HRP), Psychological Climate, Job satisfaction	OCB	At plant level: HR practices are positively & significantly related with Job satisfaction but negatively with OCB. At individual level: Psychological climate is positively & significantly associated with job satisfaction & OCB.

(Contd…)

(1)	(2)	(3)	(4)
Wang (2010)	Perceived organizational support, HRM practices	Service oriented OCB	Positive relationship between all the variables
Khan, Afzal and Zia (2010)	OCB (civic virtue, conscientiousness & altruism)	Organizational performance	Positive relationship between the variables
Saraswathi (2010)	HRD climate	–	HRD climate is better in software organizations as compared to the manufacturing organizations.
Karthikeyan, Karthi and Graf (2010)	Training program	–	Training was found very effective and overall effectiveness of training programmes contribute to growth and results of the banks.
Bulut and Culha (2010)	Organizational training	Employee commitment	All dimensions of training viz., motivation for training, access to training, benefits from training and support for training positively affected employee commitment.
Cho and Faerman (2010)	Structural and psychological empowerment	Organizational individualism and collectivism, In-role and extra-role performance	Psychological empowerment mediates the relationship between structural empowerment and extra-role performance. Organizational collectivism moderates the relationship between psychological empowerment and extra-role performance.
Baral and Bhargava (2010)	Work-life balance (job characteristics, work-life benefits and policies, supervisor support and work-family culture)	Job satisfaction, affective commitment and organizational citizenship behaviour	Supervisor support and work-family culture were positively related to job satisfaction and affective commitment. No significant association was found between work-life benefits and policies and any of the job outcome measures. Job characteristics and supervisor support were positively related to work-to-family enrichment.

(Contd...)

(1)	(2)	(3)	(4)
Snape and Redman (2010)	HRM practices	Individual employee attitudes and behavior viz., perceived job influence, perceived organizational support, OCB, in-role behaviour	HRM practices had a positive association with compliance & altruism mediated by job influence, Significant association between HRM practices & organizational support but no association was found between perceived. organizational support & OCB.
Solkhe and Chaudhary (2011)	HRD climate, OCTAPAC culture	Job satisfaction (JS) (Organizational performance)	Positive impact of HRDC & OCTAPAC on JS.
Jain and Premkumar (2011)	HRD practices	Productivity	Positive relationship between HRD practices & productivity.
Chaudhary, Rangnekar and Barua (2011)	HRD climate	Employee engagement	Positive and significant relationship between HRDC & employee engagement.
Shrivastava and Purang (2011)	Fairness of PAS and performance appraisal satisfaction	–	Private sector bank employees perceive greater fairness and satisfaction with their performance appraisal system as compared to public sector bank employees.
Jiang, Sun, and Law (2011)	Empowerment practices, Organizational structure	Job satisfaction	Positive relationship between all the variables.
Zaman Ahmad (2011)	Availability of training, support for training, motivation to learn, training environment and perceived benefits of training	OCB	Positive relationship between training variables viz., support for training, motivation to learn, training environment and benefits of training and OCB.
Vasugi, Kaviatha and Prema (2011)	Employee Empowerment	–	Employee participation in decision making, and handing more responsibility and authority to employee were found as best practices in empowerment.

(Contd...)

(1)	(2)	(3)	(4)
Sharma and Kaur (2011)	Psychological empowerment	Organizational effectiveness	Employees of the public sector banks perceived themselves to be more empowered and their organizations to be more effective than the private sector employees. For the public sector banks skills and knowledge and for the private sector banks reward system are most highly correlated with organizational effectiveness.
Chawla and Sondhi (2011)	Work-life balance	–	Organizational commitment, job autonomy and perceived work overload are strong contributors to a sense of balance for an employee.
Saxena (2011)	Pre-training, pro-training and post-training factors	Training effectiveness	Pre-training, pro-training and post-training factors lead to training effectiveness and training programmes were found highly effective.
Akinyemi (2012)	HRD Climate (HRDC)	OCB VTI	Positive relationship between HRDC & OCB Negative relationship between HRDC & VTI
Thiagrajan and Kubendran (2012)	OCB	–	Factors of OCB identified are: helping behaviour, sportsmanship, organizational loyalty, organizational compliance, individual initiative and civic virtue.
Shrivastava and Purang (2012)	Age	Fairness of performance appraisal system (PAS)	Public sector – Positive linear relationship between age & PAS. Private sector- Negative linear relationship between age & PAS.

(Contd…)

(1)	(2)	(3)	(4)
Kilam and Kumari (2012)	Career planning and HRD		Public sector banks are HRD oriented only to some extent. Corporate sector in India and the foreign banks had better career planning and HRD system as compared to Indian Public Sector Banks.
Mani and Joy (2012)	Training system	–	Training was found more effective in private sector banks as compared to public sector banks.
Kaur and Jayaraman (2012)	Training	–	Public sector bank officials highlighted training infrastructural facilities and organizational environment as the priority content, whereas the private sector banks focused on skill development and business expansion.
Mittal (2013)	HRD climate (general climate, OCTAPACE and HRD mechanisms)	–	Better general HRD climate and HRD mechanisms in public sector banks as compared to private sector banks.
Oni, Ijaiya and Mohammed (2013)	Training and management development	–	Training and management development have a positive impact on the growth of Nigeria Banking Industry.
Fujimoto, Azmat and Hartel (2013)	Work–life balance	–	Both genders (male and female) attribute a major source of their work–life conflicts to work-related matters rather than non-work matters.

Therefore, in this globally competitive and volatile external environment it has become imperative for HR professionals to foster positive, effective workplace policies and practices that focus on employee well-being, health and meaningful work and build a climate that fuels citizenship behaviours at workplaces. Organizational citizenship behaviors (OCB) are those individual behaviors that are discretionary, not directly or explicitly recognized by the formal reward system, and that in the aggregate promotes the effective functioning of the organization. Organ (1997) redefined organizational citizenship behavior as, "performance that supports the social or psychological environment in which the task performance takes place". This suggests that these behaviours could have an impact on the overall functioning of an organization by contributing to the social and psychological climate of the organizations. Based on these inputs, we propose that organizations can bring about higher levels of OCB by creating a context through progressive HRD climate and practices that fosters such behavior.

Responding to this call, an integrated model of HRD and OCB is presented in figure 10.1, grounded in social exchange theory and the norm of reciprocity, relating employees' perceptions of HRD systems to behavioral outcome of organizational citizenship behavior. From a social exchange perspective (Blau, 1964), the positive benefits of a supportive work environment enjoyed by employees obligate them to reciprocate with behaviors that benefit the organization. Therefore, it is expected that HRD climate and practices will be related to OCB. Supporting our contention is the research by Sun, Aryee, & Law, 2007 in which high-performance human resource practices are linked to service-oriented organization citizenship behaviour. Their study showed that HR practices were related to service oriented OCB and to the organization performance indicators of turnover and productivity. In this book, it is proposed that HRD climate and selected HRD practices viz., performance appraisal, employee empowerment, employee training, organizational justice, and work-life balance serve as a broad-based influence on citizenship behaviour among employees which leads to improved organizational performance.

HRD Climate and OCB: When employees evaluate their work environments in a positive way, they tend to enhance their identification with their jobs and organizations, and thus are more likely to display extra-role behaviors that are beneficial for their employers (Wei *et al.*, 2010). This indicates that general HRD climate perceptions may be strongly related to OCB, since strong positive climate perceptions may lead to obvious behavioral responses from the employees. In an empirical study of Nigerian public sector banks, Akinyemi (2012) found significant relationship between HRD climate and OCB. He suggests that for service-oriented industries, such as banks, to enhance employees' citizenship behaviour a congenial developmental climate must exist. Results from another empirical study

(Biswas, 2010) show that psychological climate is the antecedent of organizational citizenship behaviour. OCB is found to be significantly related to group cohesiveness and organizational support (Podsakoff *et al.*, 2000), which are the significant aspects of a congenial developmental climate. Similar results indicating significant relationship between organizational climate and OCB were also reported by other researchers (e.g., Pace, 2002; Aarons & Sawitzky, 2006). Therefore, based on findings of prior research, we would expect that general HRD climate of an organization would be positively related to extra-role behavior of the employees.

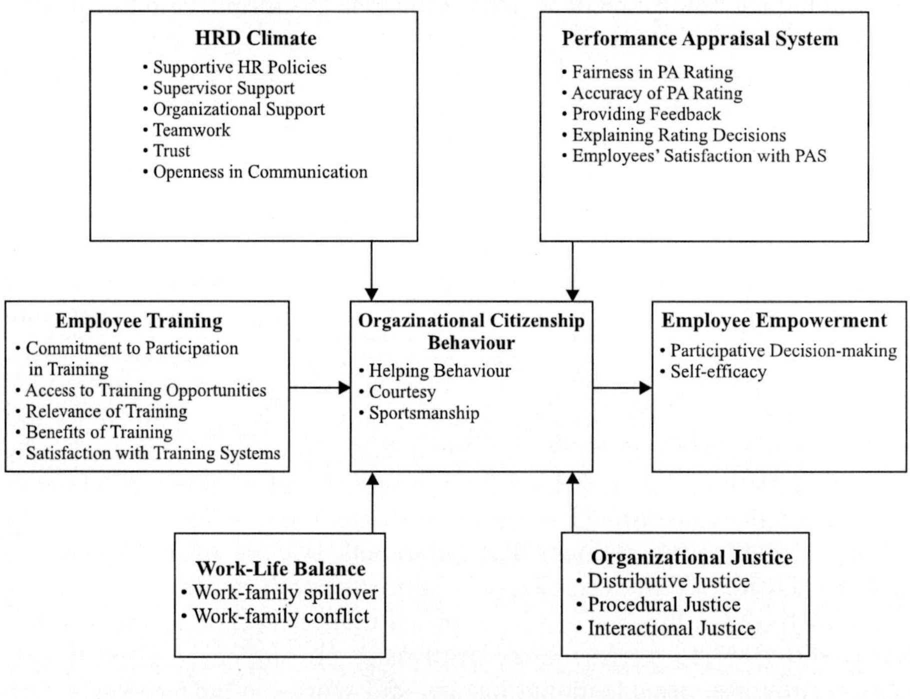

Fig. 10.1: HRD-OCB Model

Research evidence shows HR practices are strongly associated with OCB (Moorman, 1993; Deckop, Mangel & Cirka, 1999). A study by Sun, Aryee and Law (2007) revealed a partially mediating role for service oriented OCB in the relationship between high-performance human resource practices (that includes performance appraisal, training, participation among other practices) and the organizational performance indicators of turnover and productivity. HR practices such as employee empowerment and training have been determined to have a direct and positive impact on OCB (e.g., Allen & Rush 1998; Tremblay *et al.*, 1998). Given these empirical results, we predict that HRD practices selected for the study are positively related to OCB.

Performance Appraisal and OCB: Organizational citizenship behavior has been theoretically and empirically tied to performance appraisal context. But most of these studies focused on only one or two aspects of PA process. For example, Findley *et al.* (2000) found that one facet of performance appraisal context i.e., fairness in PA process explained variances in OCB. Similarly, Norris-Watts & Levy (2004) found that another dimension of performance appraisal process i.e., feedback was associated with OCB through affective commitment. However, no study is found that could relate OCB to various facets of PA process in an integrated form such as fairness, accuracy, feedback, rating decisions explanation, outcomes and satisfaction that have been conceptualized as PA process dimensions in our study.

Employee Empowerment and OCB: Employee discretion and influence through task involvement fosters a greater sense of support, trust, and intrinsic motivation and provides positive work attitudes. This increased sense of responsibility also stimulates more initiative and effort on the part of everyone involved (Appelbaum *et al.*, 2000). Morrison (1996) proposed that empowered employees are encouraged and enabled to exercise initiative and perform OCB. Employees who are empowered and satisfied would like to reciprocate by contributing performance that exceeds their role requirements. Empirically, it was found that employees would exhibit higher levels of OCB when they feel a sense of control or autonomy on the job (Wilson & Coolican, 1996). Proponents claimed that involving employees in formulating task strategies and goals promotes organizational citizenship behavior (Van Yperen *et al.*, 1999). Beauregard (2012) suggests that high self-efficacy is thought to contribute to improved performance in a range of situations due to its association with effective behavioural strategies and their empirical study clearly reported that self-efficacy had a significant positive relationship with OCB. Job self-efficacy was found to be strong predictor of organizational citizenship behavior (Todd, 2003). According to Raub & Robert (2013) employee empowerment appears to be a promising approach for service organizations seeking to stimulate higher levels of OCBs in their frontline employees. Thus, it can be said that employee empowerment has the potential to influence OCB.

Employee Training and OCB: Training has significant importance in human resource development and high levels of training opportunities will lead to superior organizational performance (Guest, 1997; Purcell, 1999). The fulfillment of employee developmental needs leads to flexible, autonomous and empowered employees based on their self-regulated behavior and discretionary effort (Arthur, 1994; Pfeffer, 1998). Dysvik and Kuwaas (2008) suggests that training opportunities serve a general purpose in making the employees feel important and taken care of in terms of having opportunities to develop. Thus, employees' positive perceptions of training and development lead to higher level of OCB. Since the training literature has witnessed only a limited amount of studies investigating the relationship between perceptions of training and work attitudes (Santos & Stuart, 2003) and behavior such as OCB, we propose to explore the relationship between training and citizenship behavior.

Organizational Justice and OCB: Greenberg (1990) described organizational justice as a literature 'grown around attempts to describe and explain the role of fairness as a consideration in the workplace'. Such perceptions can influence attitudes or behaviours for good or bad, thereby having a positive or negative impact on employee performance and organization's success. Moorman (1991) studied the relationship between fairness perceptions in the form of procedural justice and distributive justice and OCB and found a causal relationship between procedural justice and OCB but perceptions of distributive justice were not found to influence OCB. Niehoff and Moorman (1993) found significant relationship between interactional justice and sportsmanship dimension of OCB. Moorman, Niehoff and Organ (1993) found significant relationship between perceptions of procedural justice and OCB dimensions of courtesy, sportsmanship and conscientiousness. Dickinson (2009) studied the relationship between OCB and interactional justice among bank employees in US and found significant but negative correlation between OCB and interactional justice. Schappe (1998) studied the influence of job satisfaction, organizational commitment and fairness perceptions in the form of procedural justice and interactional justice on OCB and found that neither procedural justice nor interactional justice was a significant predictor of OCB. Aquino (1995) in an empirical study proved the linkages between interpersonal justice and helping behavior among both managerial and non-managerial employees in several organizations. Colquitt (2001) suggests that individual referenced type of extra role behavior (such as helping) would be driven primarily by interactional justice whereas system referenced types of extra role behavior (e.g., civic virtue) would be driven by procedural justice. Relevant literature clearly reported a strong relationship between perceptions of procedural and distributive justice and OCB in a variety of studies (e.g., Moorman, Blakely, & Niehoff, 1998; Fahr, Podsakoff, & Organ, 1990; Konovsky & Pugh, 1994; Moorman, Niehoff, & Organ, 1993; Organ & Moorman, 1993). Thus, justice perception may influence employees' opinions that they are valued by their organizations and in return, they may likely to reciprocate by performing extra role behaviours beyond the in-role requirements of their job. Most of the findings (e.g., Moorman, 1991) in this context suggest that procedural and interactional justice may influence OCB independent of any influence it has on perceptions of distributive justice. However, in this text it is argued that all the three dimension of OJ together influence OCB of employees.

Work-life Balance and OCB: Intrusion of work demands into personal life (e.g., working during the week-end) leads to heightened stress and emotional exhaustion for employees (Hyman *et al.*, 2003). Hughes and Bozioneles (2007) reported a clear connection between problems with work-life balance and withdrawal behaviours, including turnover and non-genuine sick absence. From the social exchange perspective, Lambert (2000) suggested that the perception of good benefits was related to increased participation at work and OCBs such as interpersonal helping and submission of suggestion behavior. An employee's work life balance may get imbalanced in two situations, firstly, if an employee organizational climate is such that it demands spending too much time at work, it would cause him to spend less time at his home with the family. Second, it is also a possibility that employees experiencing lots of stress at home, this may cause them to spend more time at work to escape their stressful home life. In both the situations, their work-life balance could get disturbed inhibiting them to perform extra role behavior. Thus, organizational practices which facilitate their employees to maintain a good work life balance could increase their extra role behavior.

CHAPTER 11

Measuring HRD Practices and OCB in Indian and Foreign Banks
A Study

HR practices have significant effect on organizational performance outcomes such as productivity, job satisfaction, turnover intentions, employee engagement, organizational commitment and organizational citizenship behaviour. The conceptual framework and review of past studies discussed in the previous chapters indicates toward the crucial role of HR practices in effective organizational performance. While there are evidences of assessing HRD climate and its relationship with business and individual outcomes in Indian context, our understanding and identification of the processes or mechanisms through which HRD as a function affect individual behaviour is still less explored. Moreover, one finds little evidence of research globally on the impact of HRD practices on emerging theme like organizational citizenship behaviour. The review work clearly establishes the significance of specific HRD practices suggesting that an integrated measure of human resource development systems of an organization should assess development oriented performance appraisal, training opportunities, employee empowerment mechanisms, organizational justice and work-life balance of its employees. Such human resource practices foster employees' shared perceptions of a supportive developmental climate that motivates discretionary behaviors that contribute to the organizational performance. The study will simultaneously determine the influence of HRD climate, performance appraisal, employee training, work-life balance, and organizational justice on organizational citizenship behaviour. Previous research has examined only sub-sets of these dimensions and none have theoretically integrated all these mechanisms in a single study. Based on the integrated HRD-OCB model discussed in the previous chapter, it is posited in this study that HRD climate and practices serve as a broad-based influence on citizenship behaviour among employees which leads to improved organizational performance. This study will provide a unique combination of factors affecting organizational citizenship behaviors that have not been previously studied together.

The domino effect of liberalization-privatization-globalization and the advances in information and communication technology have major HR implications for Indian banking sector as well. This scenario has forced the banking industry in India, which is largely public sector, to compete with not only the indigenous private banks but also with the foreign banks operating in India. Simultaneously, it is not an easy ride for private sector and foreign banks to challenge the prima donna status of public sector banks in India. How well these challenges are met will mainly depend on the extent to which banks leverage their human resources in the context of changing economic and business environment. Human Resources development and their attitudes and behaviour have therefore been identified as a crucial determinant of success in the banking sector and hence there is a growing interest in the effective management and development of human resources. A number of observations have been made in earlier research (e.g., Shrivastava & Purang, 2012, 2011; Akinyemi, 2012; Saxena & Tiwari, 2009; Dickinson, 2009; Priyadarshini & Venkatapathy, 2003, etc.) as regards to HRD climate, specific HRD practices and OCB in the banking industry in India and other countries, but there is dearth of studies which addressed simultaneous assessment and comparison of HRD climate, selected HRD practices and OCB and further the relationship between these variables among public sector banks, private sector banks and also foreign banks operating in India. The present study has been an endeavour to address this research gap.

Objectives of the Study

The present study was undertaken with the main purpose of studying Human Resource Development (hereafter, HRD) climate and HRD practices in selected Indian and Foreign banks and also to assess their impact on organizational citizenship behavior (hereafter, OCB) of the employees. More specifically the study was carried out to fulfill the following objectives:

1. To study the Human Resource Development (HRD) climate and practices prevailing in the selected Indian banks (public sector and private sector) and Foreign banks;
2. To understand the inter-relationship between selected HRD practices viz., Performance Appraisal, Training, Employee Empowerment and Quality of Work Life (with focus on work-life balance and organizational justice);

3. To compare between HRD practices prevailing in selected public sector and private sector banks in India;
4. To compare between HRD practices prevailing in Indian and foreign banks in India;
5. To examine OCB of the employees of selected public sector and private sector banks in India and those of the foreign banks;
6. To understand the inter-relationship between various dimensions of OCB;
7. To compare between OCB of the employees of public sector banks and that of private sector banks;
8. To compare between OCB of the employees of Indian banks and that of foreign banks in India;
9. To determine the impact of HRD climate and practices prevailing in the Indian public and private sector banks on OCB of their employees;
10. To determine the impact of HRD climate and practices prevailing in the foreign banks on OCB of their employees.

Sampling Design

The present research work is by and large empirical in nature and is based on the sample survey of managers belonging to various banking sectors as regards to the various HRD practices and their organizational citizenship behaviour. Both Indian as well as foreign banks (operating in India) viz., State Bank of India, Bank of India, ICICI Bank, HDFC Bank, Axis Bank, Yes Bank, Standard Chartered Bank, and HSBC have been selected for this study. The first two banks represent Indian public sector banks, next four banks represent Indian private sector banks and remaining two banks represent foreign banks operating in India. The selection of administrative offices/branch offices for the survey was based on convenience sampling. The administrative offices and branch offices of the selected banks were chosen from the three districts (viz., Bhopal, Indore and Ujjain) from the state of Madhya Pradesh.

The selection of managers of various cadres for the survey is based on stratified sampling. The three levels of bank managers, viz., senior managers, middle-level managers, and junior managers working in various administrative offices as well as branches of the chosen banks were selected for the purpose of the survey.

Both primary as well as secondary data from cross sections have been collected for the study. Primary data have been collected through the survey of managers of selected Indian public sector banks, Indian private sector banks and foreign banks operating in India. The questionnaires were distributed in various branches/administrative offices of the selected banks in three different cities, viz., Bhopal, Indore and Ujjain. The survey was completed throughout a period of six months, starting from April to September, 2013. Out of 450 questionnaires, three hundred and thirty-five completed or partially completed questionnaires were received, of which seventeen questionnaires were unusable due to inadequate responses. A total of 318 surveys were used in the data analyses. The response rate was 74%. Out of 318 participant managers, one hundred and thirty-six (42.7%) managers were from selected Indian public sector banks (SBI and BOI); one hundred and twenty-five (39.3%) managers were from selected Indian private sector banks (ICICI, HDFC, Axis, Yes bank); and fifty seven (18%) managers were from selected foreign banks operating in India (HSBC and Standard Chartered bank) have been included in the survey. Due care is taken in selecting managers of various cadres so as to ensure fair representation from the three levels of management. The sample included 12.3% senior level managers, 36.8% middle level managers and 50.9% junior level managers.

Respondents of the survey represented different age groups, educational qualification and experience levels. The average age of the members of the final sample was 35 years and these respondents had total experience for an average of 10.9 years. Seventy-five percent of the sample managers were male and twenty-five percent were female managers. Eighty-one percent of managers were married and nineteen percent were unmarried. Thirty-two percent of the respondents in the final sample indicated a graduate degree, sixty-eight percent were holding a post graduate degree. Out of the total respondents, around sixty-five percent were holding some or other professional degree which includes, thirty-eight percent MBA, three percent CA/CS/ICWA, five percent engineers, nineteen percent other qualifications such as law, CAIIB, etc.

Tools used for Data Collection

The present research work used primary as well as secondary data to study the HRD climate, HRD practices and organizational citizenship behavior in the banking sector in India. In order to develop the conceptual base for the study, the relevant literature and earlier researches have been referred. The sources of secondary data mainly include: research papers, published and unpublished dissertations, articles from conference proceedings, books, etc. Secondary data were also collected from the websites, annual reports, performance appraisal forms and other published and unpublished documents of the selected banks. However, the study is mainly based on primary data which were collected from senior level, middle level and junior level managers belonging to the selected banks.

The primary data were primarily collected through a survey questionnaire (Likert type scale) specifically designed for the purpose of study. The survey questionnaire consists of two sections: section 1 includes demographic questions and section 2 includes items related to study variables on five-point Likert type scale with possible responses ranging from (1) strongly disagree to (5) strongly agree. However, in additions, primary data were also collected with the help of an interview questionnaire designed to gain a better understanding of two variables viz., the performance appraisal system and employee training practices in the selected banks. It consists of open and close ended questions. Sixteen senior managers from the three different types of banks were interviewed and their responses were recorded. From each bank, two senior managers were interviewed in order to avoid any ambiguities and collect accurate information.

The following scales/sub-scales were used in the survey questionnaire administered to 318 managers of the selected banks for the purpose of collecting primary data for the study:

1. HRD Climate Sub-scale (09 items) partially adapted from HRD Scale developed by T. V. Rao and E. Abraham (1986).
2. Performance Appraisal Scale (09 items) developed by the researcher in consultation with the subject experts.
3. Employee Empowerment Scale
   (a) Participative Decision-making Sub-scale (04 items) developed by Nyhan, 1994.
   (b) Self-Efficacy Sub-scale (09 items) partially adapted from Personal Efficacy Beliefs Scale (six items) developed by Riggs, Warka, Babasa, Betancourt, & Hooker (1994); and from New General Self Efficacy Scale (three items) developed by Chen *et al* (2001)
4. Employee Training Scale (10 items) developed by researcher in consultation with the subject experts.
5. Work-Life Balance Scale (09 items) partially adapted from the scale developed by Maume and Houston (2001) and Frone and Yardley, (1996) and four items developed by researcher in consultation with the subject experts.
6. Organizational Justice Scale
   (a) Distributive Justice Sub-scale (03 items) adapted from the Organizational Justice Scale developed by Niehoff and Moorman (1993).
   (b) Procedural Justice Sub-scale (03 items) adapted from the Organizational Justice Scale (formal Procedures) developed by Niehoff and Moorman (1993).

(c) Interactional Justice Sub-scale (03 items) adapted from the Organizational Justice Scale (Formal Procedures) developed by Niehoff and Moorman (1993).

7. Organizational Citizenship Behaviour Scale

(a) Helping Behaviour Sub-scale (06 items) partially adapted from the scales developed by Podsakoff and colleagues (Podsakoff *et al.*, 1990; Podsakoff & MacKenzie, 1994); Williams and Anderson (1991) and Rego, (1999)

(b) Courtesy Sub-scale (06 items) partially developed by the researcher and partly adapted from the scales developed by Podsakoff, Ahearne and MacKenzie (1997); Williams and Anderson (1991) and Rego (1999).

(c) Sportsmanship Sub-scale (06 items) partially adapted from the Interpersonal Harmony Subscale and Personal Initiative Subscale developed by Rego (1999); Pattanayak, Misra and Niranjana (2003).

Reliability Test of the Scales Used in the Study

The reliability of the above mentioned scales/sub-scales has been tested and the reliability coefficient (Cronbach's Alpha, á) scores for the above mentioned scales/sub-scales as given below, confirmed the overall reliability of questionnaire/scales/sub-scales used in the present study.

HRD Climate (09 items) - .90; **Performance Appraisal** (09 items) - .91; **Employee Empowerment** (09 items) -.72; Participative Decision Making (04 items) - .82; Self – Efficacy - .70; **Employee Training** (10 items) - .89; **Work-Life Balance** (09 items) - .75; **Organizational Justice** (09 items) - .86; Distributive Justice (03 items) - .79; Procedural Justice (03 items) - .73; Interactional Justice (03 items) - .85; **OCB** (18 items) - .85; Helping Behaviour (06 items) - .78; Courtesy (06 items) - .87; Sportsmanship (06 items) - .60.

Tools Used for Data Analysis

Statistical tools such as arithmetic mean, standard deviation, t-test, Karl Pearson's coefficient of correlation, ANOVA and regression analysis have been used to analyze the collected data. Data analysis was carried out using statistical software SPSS.

Key Variables Studied

The data collected for the purpose of study pertain to three main variables, (1) HRD climate, (2) HRD practices and (3) OCB. An outline of key variables studied in the present research work is as follows:

1. HRD Climate: Following dimensions of HRD climate were selected for the study: (i) Supportive HR policies, (ii) Superior or supervisor support, (iii) Organizational support, (iv) Teamworking, (vi) Trust, and (vii) Open communication.
2. HRD Practices: Following HRD practices were selected for the study:
   2.1 Performance Appraisal: Following dimensions of performance appraisal were selected for the study: a) Design & implementation of PA system, and b) Employee reactions/perceptions viz., (i) Performance improvement and employee development; (ii) Fairness of PA rating; (iii) Accuracy of PA rating; (iv) Providing feedback; (v) Explaining rating decisions; (vi) Overall satisfaction with appraisal system.
   2.2 Employee Training: Following dimensions of employee training were selected for the study: a) General training practices in the selected banks, and b) Managerial perceptions of employee training with respect to: (i) Commitment to training participation, (ii) Access to training opportunities, (iii) Relevance of training to their current and future job role, (iv) Perceived usefulness or benefits of training and (v) Satisfaction with the training.
   2.3 Employee Empowerment: Following dimensions of employee empowerment were selected for the study: (i) Participative decision- making, (ii) Self-efficacy.
   2.4 Organizational Justice: Following dimensions of organizational justice were selected for the study: (i) Distributive justice, (ii) Procedural justice, (iii) Interactional justice.
   2.5 Work-Life Balance: Following dimensions of work-life balance were selected for the study: (i) Work-family spillover, (ii) Work-family conflict, (iii) Work-family facilitation.
3. Organizational Citizenship Behaviour: Following dimensions of organizational citizenship behaviour were selected for the study: (i) Helping behaviour, (ii) Courtesy and (iii) Sportsmanship.

Summary of the Main Findings

The key findings of the present study pertaining to the analysis of HRD climate, selected HRD practices and organizational citizenship behaviour based on the perceptions of the managers of the selected Indian public sector banks, Indian private sector banks and foreign banks operating in India have been summarized as under:

Exhibit 11.1

A Glance at the Main Findings Pertaining to HRD Climate

HRD Climate (HRDC) Dimensions	Overall Level of HRDC Dimension	Significance of Correlation with other dimensions*	Level of HRDC Dimensions (Gender-wise) Assessment)		Whether difference is significant (sig.) or not*	Level of HRDC Dimensions (Managerial Level-wise Assessment)			Whether difference is significant (sig.) or not	Level of HRDC Dimensions (Banking Sector-wise Assessment)			Whether difference is significant (sig.) or not**
			Males	Females		Senior Level	Middle Level	Junior Level		Public Sector	Private Sector	Foreign Banks	
Supportive HR Policies	Moderate	Significant	Moderate	Moderate	Not Sig.	High	Moderate	Moderate	Not Sig.	Moderate	Moderate	Moderate	Not Sig.
Supervisor Support	Moderate	Significant	Moderate	Moderate	Not Sig.	High	Moderate	Moderate	Not Sig.	Moderate	Moderate	Moderate	Not Sig.
Organizational Support	Moderate	Significant	Moderate	Moderate	Sig.	High	Moderate	Moderate	Not Sig.	Moderate	Moderate	Moderate	Not Sig.
Teamwork	Moderate	Significant	Moderate	Moderate	Sig.	High	Moderate	Moderate	Not Sig.	Moderate	Moderate	High	Not Sig.
Trust	Moderate	Significant	High	Moderate	Not Sig.	High	Moderate	Moderate	Not Sig.	High	Moderate	Moderate	Sig.
Openness in Communication	Moderate	Significant	Moderate	Moderate	Not Sig.	High	Moderate	Moderate	Not Sig.	Moderate	Moderate	Moderate	Not Sig.
Overall HRD Climate	Moderate	Significant	Moderate	Moderate	Not Sig.	High	Moderate	Moderate	Not Sig.	Moderate	Moderate	Moderate	Not Sig.

Note: (i) *Correlation is significant at the 0.01 level (2-tailed).

(ii) **Significant at 0.05 level of significance.

Exhibit 11.2

A Glance at the Main Findings Pertaining to Performance Appraisal (PA) Reactions

Performance Appraisal (PA) Reactions	Overall Level of PA Reactions	Significance of Correlation with other dimensions*	Level of PA Reactions (Gender-wise) Assessment)		Whether difference is significant (sign.) or not**	Level of PA Reactions (Managerial Level-wise) Assessment)			Whether difference is significant (sig.) or not*	Level of PA Reactions (Banking Sector-wise) Assessment)			Whether difference is significant (sig.) or not**
			Males	Females		Senior Level	Middle Level	Junior Level		Public Sector	Private Sector	Foreign Banks	
Performance Improvement	Moderate	Significant	Moderate	Moderate	Not Sig.	High	Moderate	Moderate	Not Sig.	High	Moderate	Moderate	Not Sig.
Employee Development	Moderate	Significant	Moderate	Moderate	Not Sig.	High	Moderate	Moderate	Not Sig.	Moderate	Moderate	Moderate	Not Sig.
Fairness in PA Rating	Moderate	Significant	Moderate	Moderate	Not Sig.	Moderate	Moderate	Moderate	Not Sig.	Moderate	Moderate	Moderate	Not Sig.
Accuracy of PA Rating	Moderate	Significant	Moderate	Moderate	Not Sig.	High	Moderate	Moderate	Sig.	Moderate	Moderate	Moderate	Not Sig.
Providing Feedback	Moderate	Significant	Moderate	Moderate	Not Sig.	Moderate	Moderate	Moderate	Not Sig.	Moderate	Moderate	Moderate	Sig.
Explaining Rating Decisions	Moderate	Significant	Moderate	Moderate	Not Sig.	Moderate	Moderate	Moderate	Not Sig.	Moderate	Moderate	Moderate	Sig.
Overall Satisfaction with PA system	Moderate	Significant	Moderate	Moderate	Not Sig.	Moderate	Moderate	Moderate	Not Sig.	Moderate	Moderate	Moderate	Not Sig.
Overall PA Reactions	Moderate	Significant	Moderate	Moderate	Not Sig.	Moderate	Moderate	Moderate	Not Sig.	Moderate	Moderate	Moderate	Not Sig.

Note: (i) *Correlation is significant at the 0.01 level (2-tailed).

(ii) **Significant at 0.05 level of significance.

Exhibit 11.3

A Glance at the Main Findings Pertaining to Employee Empowerment (EE)

Dimensions of Employee Empowerment	Overall Level of EE	Significance of Correlation with other dimensions*	Level of EE (Gender-wise Assessment)		Whether difference is significant (sig.) or not**	Level of EE (Management Level-wise Assessment)			Whether difference is significant (sig.) or not**	Level of EE (Banking Sector-wise Assessment)			Whether difference is significant (sig.) or not**
			Males	Females		Senior Level	Middle Level	Junior Level		Public Sector	Private Sector	Foreign Banks	
Participative Decision Making	Moderate	Significant	Moderate	Moderate	Not Sig.	Moderate	Moderate	Moderate	Not Sig.	Moderate	Moderate	Moderate	Not Sig.
Self-Efficacy	Moderate	Significant	Moderate	Moderate	Not Sig.	Moderate	Moderate	Moderate	Not Sig.	Moderate	Moderate	Moderate	Sig.
Overall Employee Empowerment	Moderate	Significant	Moderate	Moderate	Not Sig.	Moderate	Moderate	Moderate	Not Sig.	Moderate	Moderate	Moderate	Not Sig.

Note: (i) *Correlation is significant at the 0.01 and 0.05 level (2-tailed).

(ii) **Significant at 0.05 level of significance.

Exhibit 11.4

A Glance at the Main Findings Pertaining to Employee Training (ET)

Dimensions of Employee Training	Overall Level of ET	Significance of Correlation with other dimensions*	Level of ET (Gender-wise Assessment)		Whether difference is significant (sig.) or not**	Level of ET (Managerial Level-wise Assessment)			Whether difference is significant (sig.) or not*	Level of ET (Banking Sector-wise Assessment			Whether difference is significant (sig.) or not**
			Males	Females		Senior Level	Middle Level	Junior Level		Public Sector	Private Sector	Foreign Banks	
Commitment to Training Participation	High	Significant	High	High	Not Sig.	High	High	High	Not Sig.	High	High	Moderate	Not Sig.
Access to Training Opportunities	Moderate	Significant	Moderate	Moderate	Not Sig.	Moderate	Moderate	Moderate	Not Sig.	Moderate	Moderate	Moderate	Not Sig.
Relevance of Training	Moderate	Significant	Moderate	Moderate	Not Sig.	Moderate	Moderate	Moderate	Not Sig.	Moderate	Moderate	Moderate	Not Sig.
Benefits of Training	Moderate	Significant	High	Moderate	Not Sig.	High	Moderate	Moderate	Not Sig.	High	Moderate	Moderate	Not Sig.
Satisfaction with Training	Moderate	Significant	High	Moderate	Not Sig.	High	Moderate	Moderate	Not Sig.	High	Moderate	Moderate	Not Sig.
Overall Employee Training	Moderate	Significant	Moderate	Moderate	Not Sig.	Moderate	Moderate	Moderate	Not Sig.	Moderate	Moderate	Moderate	Not Sig.

Note: (i) *Correlation is significant at the 0.01 level (2-tailed).

(ii) **Significant at 0.05 level of significance.

Exhibit 11.5a

A Glance at the Main Findings Pertaining to Organizational Justice (OJ)

Dimensions of Organizational Justice	Overall Level of OJ	Significance of Correlation with other dimensions*	Level of OJ (Gender-wise Assessment)		Whether difference is significant (sig.) or not**	Level of OJ (Managerial Level-wise Assessment)			Whether difference is significant (sig.) or not*	Level of OJ (Banking Sector-wise Assessment)			Whether difference is significant (sig.) or not**
			Males	Females		Senior Level	Middle Level	Junior Level		Public Sector	Private Sector	Foreign Banks	
Distributive Justice	Moderate	Significant	Moderate	Moderate	Not Sig.	Moderate	Moderate	Moderate	Not Sig.	Moderate	Moderate	Moderate	Sig.
Procedural Justice	Moderate	Significant	Moderate	Moderate	Not Sig.	Moderate	Moderate	Moderate	Not Sig.	Moderate	Moderate	Moderate	Sig.
Interactional Justice	Moderate	Significant	Moderate	Moderate	Sig.	Moderate	Moderate	Moderate	Not Sig.	Moderate	Moderate	Moderate	Not Sig.
Overall Organizational Justice	Moderate	Significant	Moderate	Moderate	Not Sig.	Moderate	Moderate	Moderate	Not Sig.	Moderate	Moderate	Moderate	Sig.

Note: (i) *Correlation is significant at the 0.01 level (2-tailed).

(ii) **Significant at 0.05 level of significance.

Exhibit 11.5b

A Glance at the Main Findings Pertaining to Work-Life Balance (WLB)

Dimensions of Work-Life Balance (WLB)	Overall Level of WLB	Significance of Correlation with other dimensions*	Level of WLB (Gender-wise Assessment)		Whether difference is significant (sig.) or not**	Level of WLB (Managerial Level-wise Assessment)			Whether difference is significant (sig.) or not*	Level of WLB (Banking Sector-wise Assessment)			Whether difference is significant (sig.) or not**
			Males	Females		Senior Level	Middle Level	Junior Level		Public Sector	Private Sector	Foreign Banks	
Work-Family Spillover	Low	Significant	Low	Low	Not Sig.	Low	Low	Low	Not Sig.	Low	Low	Low	Sig.
Work-Family Conflict	Moderate	Significant	Moderate	Moderate	Not Sig.	Moderate	Moderate	Moderate	Not Sig.	Moderate	Moderate	Moderate	Sig.
Work-Family Facilitation	Moderate	Significant	Moderate	Moderate	Not Sig.	Moderate	Moderate	Moderate	Not Sig.	Moderate	Moderate	Moderate	Sig.
Overall Work-Life balance	Moderate	Significant	Moderate	Moderate	Not Sig.	Moderate	Moderate	Moderate	Not Sig.	Moderate	Moderate	Moderate	Sig.

Note: (i) *Correlation is significant at the 0.01 level (2-tailed).

(ii) **Significant at 0.05 level of significance

Exhibit 11.6

A Glance at the Main Findings Pertaining to Organizational Citizenship Behaviour (OCB)

Dimensions of Organizational Citizenship Behaviour	Overall Level of OCB	Significance of Correlation with other dimensions*	Level of OCB (Gender-wise Assessment)		Whether difference is significant (sig.) or not**	Level of OCB (Managerial Level-wise Assessment)			Whether difference is significant (sig.) or not*	Level of OCB (Banking Sector-wise Assessment)			Whether difference is significant (sig.) or not**
			Males	Females		Senior Level	Middle Level	Junior Level		Public Sector	Private Sector	Foreign Banks	
Helping Behaviour	Moderate	Significant	Moderate	Moderate	Not Sig.	High	Moderate	Moderate	Not Sig.	Moderate	Moderate	Moderate	Not Sig.
Courtesy	High	Significant	High	High	Not Sig.	High	High	High	Not Sig.	High	High	Moderate	Sig.
Sportsmanship	Moderate	Significant	Moderate	Moderate	Not Sig.	Moderate	Moderate	Moderate	Not Sig.	Moderate	Moderate	Moderate	Sig.
Overall OCB	Moderate	Significant	Moderate	Moderate	Not Sig.	Moderate	Moderate	Moderate	Not Sig.	Moderate	Moderate	Moderate	Sig.

Note: (i) *Correlation is significant at the 0.01 level (2-tailed).

(ii) **Significant at 0.05 level of significance.

Exhibit 11.7

A Glance at the Main Findings Pertaining to Relationship between Specific Dimensions of HRD and Organizational Citizenship Behaviour (OCB)

Various HRD Dimensions	Extent to which the HRD Dimension Exists	Significance of Correlation with OCB*	Impact of HRD Dimension on OCB
HRD Climate (HRDC)	Moderate	Significant	Significant
Performance Appraisal (PA)	Moderate	Significant	Significant
Employee Empowerment (EE)	Moderate	Significant	Significant
Employee Training (ET)	Moderate	Significant	Significant
Work-Life Balance (WLB)	Moderate	Not Significant	Not Significant
Organizational Justice (OJ)	Moderate	Significant	Not Significant

Note: (i) *Correlation is significant at the 0.01 level (2-tailed).

Recommendations

Prior empirical research has provided considerable evidences that the extent of HR initiatives by the organizations directly influence the social exchange relationships between the employee and organization which ultimately affect the firm performance (e.g., Pare & Trembley, 2007; Seidu, 2011). Such social exchange relationships have consistently proven to be a significant predictor of organizational citizenship behavior which further predicts service quality and organizational performance. Therefore, it is suggested that organizations in general and Indian banks in particular must begin to design or remodel their HRD practices in ways that not only facilitates employee development but are also influential in promoting OCBs among employees. The findings of survey results have clearly showed that HRD climate as well as selected HRD practices exists at a moderate level in the Indian public sector banks, private sector banks and foreign banks. Thus, a substantial level of improvement is warranted in the overall HRD scenario of Indian banking sector. Based on the analysis of findings, observations and interactions during the field visits, following recommendations are put forth in the context of remodeling of HRD practices in the Indian banking sector:

Supportive HRD Climate: Organizational support and supervisor support were found to highly correlate with overall HRD climate, so banks must ensure that poor or low job performers are helped in a planned way to improve their current task performance as well as to acquire new knowledge and skills. Through creating a shared belief in employee development, supervisors and senior managers play a pivotal role in establishing a development oriented climate in the banks. HR department in Indian public sector banks are required to devise supportive HR policies that facilitate employee development and employees identified with low job performance must be given proper counseling, training and coaching to improve their competence level. Similarly, Indian private sector banks cannot ignore the low levels of trust among their employees as it may lead to detrimental working relationships. In order to improve the trust level among employees, senior management must ensure transparency and objectivity in their actions and decisions and avoid any sort of nepotism. Low levels of trust among employees may affect their trust level with customers also. Here, it needs to be stressed that customization and a wide choice of services offered by technological advancement is no substitute for what customers care about most in their interactions with banks i.e., reliability, service, and an institution they can trust.

Performance Appraisal for Employee Development and Improvement: Organizations must ensure to minimize the use of performance appraisals as political tools (to favour or punish subordinates) and maximize its use as a development tool. The key objective of performance appraisals must be the development and improvement of employees and besides using it as feedback mechanism, it should be considered more as a feed-forward instrument for future corrective actions. In view of our finding of a moderate level of implementation and satisfaction with performance appraisal system in the Indian banks, the performance appraisal process should be improvised further in terms of fairness, accuracy and explanation of rating decisions. It was observed that most of the supervisors were not clearly aware of the various rating errors and therefore, proper education of supervisors on various rating errors will ensure unbiased and accurate appraisals leading to employee satisfaction with the process. Moreover, mock appraisal sessions by teaming up supervisors and HRD managers should be organized to showcase how clear and constructive feedback will help employees to build on their strengths and build up their weaker areas. Giving extra emphasis to subordinate participation in the process of goal-setting, review discussions and feedback process will further enhance the transparency of performance appraisals. Clear and time bound performance improvement plans (PIP) should be worked out for poor performers with proper monitoring to track their progress. The Indian public sector banks, in particular, should incorporate and emphasize the process of mid-term reviews to track the progress of annual performance goals and targets. Similar to foreign banks operating in India and Indian private sector banks, supervisors in the Indian public sector banks must also clearly explain the rating decisions after the appraisal process and employees must be provided at least twice –yearly developmental feedback. This would improve employee's overall satisfaction with performance appraisal system and help in developing an organization –wide performance culture within the banks.

Employee Training for Skills Development and Learning Satisfaction: Employees are more satisfied with training that is provided to them in a way they believe is most effective in helping them to learn. Most of the respondents in the present study preferred classroom training which is actually 1-2 times in a year per employee in case of the Indian public sector banks as against to 4-6 times per employee, annually, in case of the Indian private sector banks and foreign banks operating in India. It is therefore suggested that a combination of e-learning and classroom training should be preferred so that employees get basic knowledge about the topic through online modules before they do a classroom course on that topic and so it would be possible to focus more on the practical part during the classroom training. This would result in higher level of training satisfaction as well as better learning. Public sector banks, although investing substantially on training interventions and infrastructure, still employees perceive that they are not given proper access to training opportunities. Therefore, these banks must further strengthen their classroom as well as online training initiatives to expand the reach of training to widespread employee base of public sector banks. Furthermore, a systematic analysis of training needs and scientific selection of trainees before making training decisions is found missing in most of the banks. It is thus recommended that instead of top-down approach, a bottom-up approach should be followed and training must be scheduled and trainees should be nominated based on the developmental needs and requests of employees rather than managers nominating trainees based on their whims and fancies. Managers should reward trainees for successfully completing training programmes and for transferring the learning on their jobs. Finally, a learning culture needs to be developed that emphasizes the development of human resources for better individual as well as organizational performance. HRD practitioners must understand that the training and development opportunities they offer, are influential not only in the overall job satisfaction of employees but also result in shaping workplace attitudes such as OCBs which are important for overall organizational effectiveness.

Employee Empowerment for Customer Satisfaction: Empowerment initiatives must be designed in order to give more participation, autonomy and feelings of competence to employees in an organization. In order to empower team members, managers must give up some aspects of control and in return they will have more time to look at the big picture and engage in strategic thinking. In banks, it is the junior level managers who interacts more with the customers, therefore, they should be helped by coaching, training and providing necessary information to make decisions independently so as to improve their own productivity as well as customer's satisfaction. Managers must follow the rule of empowerment i.e., tell, teach and give: Tell people what they have to do, teach them how to do and give them resources they need. If organizations want their employees to feel confident of their abilities, employee should be given regular job training and support. In order to enhance the efficacy levels, managers must encourage employees to take initiatives, being creative and innovative in routine functioning and provide them constructive developmental feedback. If employees are empowered, they will feel important and they will convey these feelings to customers resulting in improved service and better performance. HR therefore, must nurture and encourage empowerment by creating an empowering environment in which employees are given goals, information, feedback, training, and perhaps most importantly, positive reinforcement.

Organizational Justice for Job Satisfaction: It is well established fact that employees may be willing to accept an unwanted result if they believe that the decision process leading up to it was fair and transparent. Give the moderate level of OJ, banks managers have to become aware of the extent their decisions and their methods of making the decisions influence the performance of their staff, and how this in turn impacts customer satisfaction. It is to be noted here that robust leader-member exchange and the quality of the supervisor's relationship with employees might be effective in creating their perceptions of fairness in outcomes and in the decision-making process. In the context of current findings, private sector banks must ensure transparency and fairness in promotion and other reward decisions and avoid favouritism as the role of procedural justice is very important as regards to personal outcome such as job satisfaction and turnover intentions. Public sector banks must improve the fairness of outcomes such as fair distribution of pay and rewards and reasonable work load as they have greater impact on outcomes like OCB. Although equality principles such as predetermined job grades and salary bands are upheld in the public sector banks to a good extent, however, due to technology advances and increased competition the nature of work and workload in these banks is not relaxed in the same way as it used to be in earlier times and employees perceive that they have heavy workloads which is not commensurate with the level of their pay. Moreover, public sector banks must strengthen their rewards and recognition policies for employees and apply such policies fairly and consistently to all employees. Employees must be rewarded based on performance and merit in order to create positive perceptions of fair treatment. Comparatively analyzing, foreign banks scored significantly highest on justice dimension among all the three type of banks and this striking feature could be a 'carrot' factor to lure experienced and talented professionals from their competitors.

Work-life Balance to Sustain Employee Retention: The perception that an organization 'cares' about its employees can affect whether they feel they have the right balance between home and work or not. Both public sector and private sector bank employees work for increasingly long hours and therefore experience more and more imbalance between personal pursuits and professional responsibilities. Here it would be worth quoting one of the anonymous respondents of our study who while discussing about their working schedule sharply commented that ...`I would never recommend my children to take up a career in banking...' The remark clearly reflects the agony of a hectic work life faced by the bankers. Banks should not neglect this issue as this may have potentially damaging consequences and results in retention problems. Thus, bank management need to offer a range of family-friendly policies to facilitate better balance between work and home and they may be required to combat a long-hours culture and increase the possibility of flexible working for all staff. Work-life balance can minimize stress and fatigue at work, enabling people to have safer and healthier working lives. Supervisor support also plays a crucial role in maintaining work-life balance. Therefore, HR should sensitize supervisors and managers to the concept of work-life balance and encourage them to offer support to their team members.

Organizational Citizenship Behaviour for Organizational Effectiveness: Studies have shown that OCB tends to exhibit positive relationships with individual outcomes (e.g., Werner, 2000; Podsakoff *et al.*, 2009) as well as organizational effectiveness and performance (e.g., Bateman & Organ, 1983; Organ, 1988; Podsakoff & MacKenzie, 1997; Nielsen, Hrivnak & Shaw, 2007). It is therefore incumbent upon management to promote OCBs in their banks. Managers must focus on job role as a means to increase the occurrence of OCB and so they must ensure that the employees perceive their tasks as autonomous, meaningful and satisfying. Through the lens of social exchange theory (Blau, 1964), employees who feel cognitively satisfied with their jobs will make an attempt to reciprocate to the organization, co-workers and customers in the form of discretionary behaviors. To encourage citizenship behaviours, supervisors should improve dyadic relationships with the employees by lending unconditional support, fair allocation of resources, opportunities and rewards and clear, transparent communication. Recent research suggests that strategically harnessing helping will become more critical to organizations in the future (Mossholder, Richardson, & Settoon, 2011). Therefore, it is important for organizations to understand and implement processes that ultimately lead employees to exchange help over time. Counseling employees about the interpersonal risks and ways of mitigating them could assist in the development of appropriate helping and courteous relationships. It is recommended for supervisors to set examples on helping, courteous and sportsmanship behaviours and develop a 'country' of good citizens for overall organizational effectiveness.

The above initiatives and/or alterations in HRD mechanisms will guarantee the development of a robust HRD orientation within the Indian banks. It would further enable individual development and subsequently facilitate employee satisfaction. A shared perception of an organization's initiation of a high-quality relationship among employees engenders a relational view of the employment relationship defined by interdependency, mutuality, and reciprocity; this view obligates them to reciprocate with service- oriented OCB (Sun, Aryee & Law, 2007). In the study, the overall impact of HRD dimensions was found significant on OCB level of the employees. More specifically, employee empowerment and training were found as the most significant predictors while organizational justice and work-life balance as the insignificant ones. As a result, HRD efforts in the form of employee training and participation in planning and decision making conveys to employees that their organization is concerned about their development and in exchange employees will be willing to do extra efforts to contribute to the organizational effectiveness. Henceforth, human resource decision makers should place a strong emphasis on employees' development for training as well as empowerment and develop a corporate culture that emphasizes 'going the extra mile' for customers, colleagues, or the organization itself thereby sustaining organizations' competitive advantages.

Directions for Future Research

Indian banking is under revision and in such times of change and challenge, it has become imperative for their HR department to effectively manage the performance and development of human resources for the achievement of competitive advantage. Although, the present study focused on a number of mechanisms that are aimed at employee development, many facets of HRD are still left unattended in the present study. Comprehensive research on HRD scenario in Indian banks may facilitate better assessment of the HRD 'big picture' and identify the roadblocks to successful development interventions in the banks. There is a need to delve into realistic HR related issues and challenges faced by Indian banking and further to provide feasible solutions to overcome the same. Such focused studies may pave the way to innovative strategies and practices for better human resource development. To enhance external validity, future research should embrace a wider population covering more geographic locations within the Indian banking environment as well as in different industry segments. Moreover, our findings reflect the perceptions of only managerial employees of the banking sector while a good number of employees, especially in the Indian public sector banks, belong to non-managerial or clerical cadre. Therefore, a more detailed investigation of HRD climate, HRD practices and OCB of non-managerial staff who were unrepresented in the present survey should be carried out. Future studies should also include the effect of demographic variables in the relationship of HRD climate, HRD practices and OCB. A number of studies have indicated that HR practices contribute towards various organizational and individual outcomes leading to the achievement of competitive advantage (Arthur 1994; Huselid 1995; Delery & Doty 1996; Bae & Lawler 2000; Dyer & Reeves 1995; Orlitzky & Frenkel 2005; Sun, Aryee & Law 2007; Jain, Premkumar & Kamble, 2013). Without any intention to discount the significance of these frameworks, it is to point out here that these studies examined generally the common traditional sets of HR practices. There are various other HR practices that influence performance of organizations such as environment that encourage creativity, transparency, open communication, good group dynamics, knowledge of growth opportunities, management trust in employees, HR philosophies, investment in people, grievance handling mechanisms, etc. which need to be addressed and at scale representative of Indian banking systems (Bhatt, 2012). Future research therefore should focus on broadening the study on HRM/HRD practices in the banking sector by studying a wider variety of HR mechanisms. The result of this work suggests that HRD dimensions contribute meaningfully to the occurrence of organizational citizenship behavior. A number of theoretical and conceptual frameworks have been proposed in earlier studies (Pare & Trembley, 2007; Sun, Aryee & Law, 2007) indicating positive HR-OCB relationship. These frameworks have similar or dissimilar sets of HR practices while analyzing linkages with OCB. Further relational studies may include a broad range of HR practices addressed in above mentioned frameworks (in addition to those studied in the present research) such as guaranteed job security, broad career paths, promotions from within, broad job description, flexible job assignment, communication, internal career opportunities, information sharing, competence development, recognition. Much of the empirical research examining OCB in organizational contexts claims causal relationships (Podsakoff *et al.*, 2000) and indeed the theoretical frameworks supporting the OCB construct explicitly incorporates the notion that OCB has positive, identifiable effects (Organ, 1988). Therefore, it is clearly required from specific empirical studies to provide substantiation for these causal assertions. Research has also shown that because extra role behavior can make an organization a more attractive place in which to work, it can enhance an organization's ability to attract and retain good employees (Podsakoff *et al.*, 2000). Thus, a high level of OCBs reflects employees' true willingness to be involved in the organization (Shore, Barkdale, & Shore, 1995; Chen, Hui, & Sego, 1998). Therefore, research on what other variables, in addition to HRD factors impact organizational citizenship behavior, and how they impact such behavior, is valuable to managers and scholars. Future studies may consider other possible predictors of OCB such as trust, leader support and personality traits (Penner, Midili, & Kegelmeyer, 1997; Podsakoff *et al.*, 2000; Bachrach, 2002; Elanain, 2007). The current study only focused upon the direct effect that HRD variables have upon OCB; however, it is also encourage studying indirect linkages that particular HRD variables may share with OCB or particular dimensions of OCB. Therefore, empirical research can be made in future to study the influence of HRD climate and HRD practices on organizational performance or effectiveness via OCB as a mediating variable since the underlying processes determining HRD - organizational performance relationship is relatively less explored area in Indian contexts. Similarly, future research may examine the potential mediators between HRD practices and organizational citizenship behaviours (for instance, psychological climate, job satisfaction, strong commitment) and OCB and organizational performance (culture, trust, service quality, for instance). Hopefully, the framework proposed in this research will stimulate future research connecting HRD and citizenship behavior and will promote greater understanding of the challenge of cultivating viable developmental climate in the organizations. Another future research recommendation stems from the findings of robust relationship specifically between employee empowerment as well as training and OCB. Scholars should now begin to investigate how empowerment interventions or training in organizations can combine to ultimately impact the citizenship behavior of the employees. From a practical stance, this field of inquiry should be attractive to managers as it would enable them to not only predict OCB through the utilization of additional training procedures or facilitation of mentoring programmes, but also even possibly augment the unique level of social capital in the organization (Bolino *et al.*, 2002). Given the notion that employee perceptions of HRD practices have these kinds of meaningful employee-focused effects as discussed above, it will be important to understand how, when and why these perceptions develop, so as to provide greater insight to practicing managers. Thus, it can be said that the scope is wide open for future studies to explore certain issues which remain unaddressed but critically raised in the present study.

Conclusion

The present study was conducted to study the level of existence of HRD climate, selected HRD practices and OCB in Indian banking sector and also to examine the impact of HRD climate and HRD practices on citizenship behavior of employees. The results of the study showed that HRD climate, selected HRD practices (performance appraisal, employee empowerment, employee training and quality of work life: organizational justice and work-life balance) and citizenship behaviours in the organizations under study were found to exist at a moderate level in the banks under study. The correlation analysis of the study variables revealed that HRD climate and HRD practices (except work-life balance) were positively and significantly correlated with OCB. Of all the study variables, employee empowerment and employee training were found to be most significant variables in terms of their impact on OCB as revealed by the multiple regression analysis. Although the other dimensions viz., HRD climate and performance appraisal are significant in terms of their impact on OCB, the impact of organizational justice and work-life balance was found to be insignificant. The overall impact of selected HRD dimensions was found significant on OCB level of the employees. This study represents a pioneer effort to study the impact of HRD climate and selected combination of HRD practices on the OCB level of employees. Hence, this research makes a significant contribution to the literature available on HRD climate, HRD practices and OCB in an Indian context.

References

Aarons, G.A., & Sawitzky, A.C. (2006). Organizational Climate Partially Mediates the Effect of Culture on Work Attitudes and Staff turnover in Mental Health Services. *Administration and Policy in Mental Health and Mental Health Service Research*, 33(3), 289-301.

Adams, J.S. (1965). Inequity in Social Exchange. In L. Berkowitz (Ed.), *Advances in Experimental Social Psychology*, Vol. 2 (pp. 267-299). New York: Academic Press.

Agarwala, T. (2002). The Practice of HRD: Internal Customers' View. *Vision: The Journal of Business Perspective*, 6 (1), 25-32.

Ahmad, K.Z., & Bakar, R.A. (2003). The Association between Training and Organizational Commitment among white-collar Workers in Malaysia. *International Journal of Training and Development*, 7 (3), 166-185.

Akinyemi B.O. (2012). Human Resource Development Climate as a Predictor of Citizenship Behaviour and Voluntary turnover Intentions in the Banking Sector. *International Business Research*, 5(1), 110-119.

Allen, T.D., & Rush, M.C. (1998). The Effects of Organizational Citizenship Behavior on Performance Judgments: A Field Study and a Laboratory Experiment. *Journal of Applied Psychology*, 83(2), 247-260.

Ambrose, M.L., & Arnaud, A. (2005). Are Procedural Justice and Distributive Justice Conceptually Distinct? In Greenberg, Jerald (Ed); Colquitt, Jason A. (Ed), (2005). *Handbook of Organizational Justice* (pp. 59-84). Mahwah, NJ, US: Lawrence Erlbaum Associates Publishers.

Ambrose, M.L., & Schminke M. (2007). Examining Justice Climate: Issues of Fit, Simplicity, and Content. R*esearch in Multi Level Issues*, 6, 397-413.

Appelbaum, E., Bailey, T., Berg, P., & Kalleberg, A. L. (2000). *Manufacturing Advantage: Why High-Performance Work Systems Pay Off.* Ithaca, NY: Cornell University Press.

Aquino, K. (1995). Relationships Among Pay Inequity, Perceptions of Procedural Justice, and Organizational Citizenship. *Employee Responsibilities and Rights Journal,* 8 (1), 21-33.

Argyris, Chris. (1998, May-June). Empowerment. The Emperor's New Clothes. *Harvard Business Review,* 76, 98-104.

Argyris, Chris. (2000). *Flawed Advice and the Management Trap.* Oxford. Oxford University Press.

Arthur, J.B. (1994). Effects of Human Resource Systems on Manufacturing Performance and turnover. *Academy of Management Journal,* 37(3), 670-687.

Bae, J., & Lawler, J.J. (2000). Organizational and HR Strategies in Korea: Impact on Firm Performance in an Emerging Economy. *Academy of Management Journal,* 43(3), 502-517.

Bacchus, M.K. (1992). *Human Resource Development: Definition, Importance and Strategies.* Common Wealth Secretariat, London.

Bakhshi, A., Kumar, K., & Rani, E. (2009). Organizational Justice Perceptions as Predictor of Job Satisfaction and Organization Commitment. *International Journal of Business and Management,* 4 (9), 145-154.

Bamberger, P., & Meshoulam, I. (2000). *Human Resource Strategy.* Newbury Park, CA: Sage.

Bandura, A. (1977). Self-Efficacy: Toward a Unifying Theory of Behavioral Change. *Psychological Bulletin,* 84(2), 191-215.

Bandura, A. (1986). *Social Foundations of thought and Action: A Social-Cognitive View.* Englewood Cliffs: Prentice Hall.

Barbuto, Jr. J.E., Brown, L.L., Wilhite, M.S., & Wheeler, D.W. (2001). Testing the Underlying Motives of Organizational Citizenship Behaviour: A Field Study of Agricultural Co-op Workers. In *28th Annual National Agricultural Educational Research Conference, New Orleans, LA* (pp. 539-553).

Barling, J., & Phillips, M. (1993). Interactional, Formal, and Distributive Justice in the Workplace: An Exploratory Study. *Journal of Psychology,* 127(6), 649-656.

Barnard, C.I. (1938). *The Functions of the Executive.* Cambridge, MA: Harvard University Press.

Bartel, A.P. (1994). Productivity Gains from the Implementation of Employee Training Programs. *Industrial Relations: A Journal of Economy and Society,* 33(4), 411-425.

Bartlett, K.R., & Kang, D. (2004). Training and Organizational Commitment Among Nurses following Industry and Organizational Change in New Zealand and the United States, *Human Resource Development International,* 7 (4), 423-440.

Bartlett, K.R. (2001). The Relationship between Training and Organizational Commitment: A Study in the Health Care Field. *Human Resource Development Quarterly,* 12 (4), 335-352.

Bateman, T.S., & Organ, D.W. (1983). Job Satisfaction and the Good Soldier: The Relationship between Affect and Employee "Citizenship". *Academy of Management Journal,* 26(4), 587-595.

Baruch, Y. (2004). *Managing Careers: Theory and Practice.* Harlow, UK: Prentice-Hall.

Beauregards, T.A. (2012). Perfectionism, Self-efficacy and OCB: The Moderating Role of Gender. *Personnel Review,* 41(5), 590-608.

Beckhard, R. (1969). *Organization Development: Strategies and Models.* Reading, MA: Addison-Wesley.

Bernardin, H.J., & Beatty R.W. (1984). *Performance Appraisal: Assessing Human Performance at Work.* Boston: Kent.

Bhatnagar, J. (2005). The Power of Psychological Empowerment as an Antecedent to Organizational Commitment in Indian Managers. *Human Resource Development International,* 8(4), 419-433.

Bhatnagar, J., & Sharma, A. (2004). The Level of Psychological Empowerment in Indian Managers, *Global Business Review,* 5(2), 217-227.

Bhatnagar, J., & Sandhu, S. (2005). Psychological Empowerment and Organizational Citizenship Behaviour in IT Managers: A Talent Retention Tool. *Indian Journal of Industrial Relations,* 40, 449-469.

Bhatt, Prachi (2012). HRD in Emerging Economies: Research Perspectives in Indian Banking. *Indian Journal of Industrial Relations,* 47 (4), 665-672.

Bies, R.J. (1986). Identifying Principles of Interactional Justice: The Case of Corporate Recruiting. In R.J. Bies (Ed.). *Moving beyond Equity Theory: New Directions in Research on Justice in Organizations.* Symposium at the Annual Meeting of the Academy of Management, Chicago, IL.

Bies, R.J., & Moag, J.F. (1986). Interactional Justice: Communication Criteria of Fairness. In R.J. Lewicki, B.H. Sheppard, & M.H. Bazerman (Eds.), *Research on Negotiations in Organizations,* Vol. 1 (pp. 43-55). Greenwich, CT: JAI Press.

Bies R.J., & Shapiro D.L. (1987). Voice and Justification: Their Influence on Procedural Fairness Judgements. *Academy of Management Journal,* 31(3), 576-665.

Bies, R.J., & Shapiro, D.L. (1987). Interactional Fairness Judgments: The Influence of Causal Accounts. *Social Justice Research*, 1 (2), 199-218.

Biswas, S. (2010). Commitment as a Mediator between Psychological Climate and Citizenship Behaviour. *Indian Journal of Industrial Relations*, 45, 411-423.

Blau, P.(1964). *Exchange and Power in Social Life*. New York: Wiley.

Blau, J.B., & R.D. Alba (1982). Empowering Nets of Participation. *Administrative Science Quarterly*, 27, 363-379.

Bogler, A., & Somech, R. (2004). Influence of Teacher Empowerment on Teachers' Organizational Commitment, Professional Commitment and Organizational Citizenship Behavior in Schools. *Teaching and Teacher Education*, 20 (3), 277-289.

Borman. W.G. (1991). Job Behavior, Performance, and Effectiveness. In M.D. Dunnette & L.M. Hough (Eds.), *Handbook of Industrial and Organizational Psychology* (2nd Ed.), Vol. 2 (pp. 271-326). Palo Alto. CA: Consulting Psychologists Press.

Borman, W.C., & Motowidlo, S.J. (1993). Expanding the Criterion Domain to include Elements of Contextual Performance. In N. Schmitt & W.C. Borman (Eds.), *Personality Selection* (pp. 71-98). San Francisco: Jossey-Bass.

Borman,W.C., Penner, L.A., Allen,T.D., & Motowidlo, S. (2001). Personality Predictors of Citizenship Performance. *International Journal of Selection and Assessment*, 9 (1-2), 52-69.

Boselie, P., Dietz, G., & Boon, C. (2005). Commonalities and Contradictions in HRM and Performance Research. *Human Resource Management Journal*, 15 (3), 67-94.

Bowen, D.E., & Lawler, E.E. (1995). Empowering Service Employees. *Sloan Management Review, Summer* 1995, 73.

Boxall, P., & Macky, K. (2009). Research and Theory on High-performance Work Systems: Processing the High Involvement Stream. *Human Resource Management Journal*, 19(1), 3-23.

Broady-Preston, Judith, & Steel, Lucy (2002). Employees, Customers and Internal Marketing Strategies in LIS. *Library Management*, 23 (8/9), 384-393.

Brown, M., & Heywood, J. S. (2005). Performance Appraisal Systems: Determinants and Change. *British Journal of Industrial Relations*, 43(4), 659-679.

Buckley, Roger, & Caple, Jim (2000). *A Systematic Approach to Training: The Theory and Practice of Training*, Kogan, Stylus Publishing Co. , 4th edition, 17-28, 269-274.

Bulut, Kagri, & Culha, Osman (2010). The Effects of Organizational Training on Organizational Commitment. *International Journal of Training and Development*, 14 (4), 309-322.

Carlson, D., & Perrewe, P. (1999). The Role of Social Support in the Stressor-strain Relationship: An Examination of Work-family Conflict. *Journal of Management*, 25 (4), 513-540.

Chaitanya, S.K. & Tripathi, N. (2001). Dimensions of Organizational Citizenship Behaviour. *Indian Journal of Industrial Relations*, 37, 217-230.

Chan, K.W., & Wyatt, T.A. (2007). Quality of Work Life: A Study of Employees in Shanghai, China. *Asia Pacific Business Review*, 13 (4), 501-517.

Chandra, S., & Coeho, S. J. (1993). *HRD News Letter*. Jan-June, p 19.

Chandrashekar, S.F. (2009). Employee Engagement as Function of HRD in NGOs: A Study of NGO's Employees in South India. *SuGyaan*, 1, 18-37.

Chaudhary, R., Rangnekar, S., & Barua, M. (2011). Relation between Human Resource Development Climate and Employee Engagement: Results from India. *Europe's Journal of Psychology*, 7(4), 664-685.

Chaudhary, R., Rangnekar, S., & Barua, M. (2012). Relationships between Occupational Self Efficacy, Human Resource Development Climate, and Work Engagement. *Team Performance Management*, 18 (7/8), 370-383.

Chien, M. (2004). An Investigation of the Relationship of Organizational Structure, Employee's Personality and Organizational Citizenship Behaviors. *Journal of American Academy of Business*, 5, 428-431.

Chisholm, R.F., & Vansina, L.S. (1993). Varieties of Participation. *Public Administration Quarterly*, 17(3), 291-315.

Choudhary, G. (2011). The Dynamics of Organizational Climate: An Exploration. *Management Insight*, VII(2), 111-116.

Cho, T., & Faerman, S.R. (2010). An Integrative Model of Empowerment and Individuals' in-role and Extra-role Performance in the Korean Public Sector: Moderating Effects of Organizational Individualism and Collectivism. *International Public Management Journal*, 13(2), 130-154.

Clark, S. (2000). Work-family Border Theory: A New Theory of Work-life Balance. *Human Relations*, 53 (6), 747-770.

Colquitt, J.A. (2001). On the Dimensionality of Organizational Justice: A Construct Validation of a measure. *Journal of Applied Psychology*, 86(3), 386-400.

Colquitt, J.A., Conlon, D.E., Wesson, M.J., Porter, C.O. L.H., & Ng, K.Y. (2001). Justice at the Millennium: A Meta-analytic Review of 25 years of Organizational Justice Research. *Journal of Applied Psychology*, 86(3), 425-445.

Conger, J.A., & Kanungo, R.N. (1998). The Empowerment Process: Integrating Theory and Practice. *Academy of Management Review,* 13, 471-482.

Cook, J., & Crossman, A. (2004). Satisfaction with Performance Appraisal Systems. *Journal of Managerial Psychology*, 19 (5), 526-541.

Cropanzano, R., & Greenberg, J. (1997). Progress in Organizational Justice: Tunneling through the Maze. In C.L. Cooper & I.T. Robertson (Eds.), *International Review of Industrial and Organisational Psychology,* Vol. 12 (pp. 317-372). Chichester, UK: Wiley.

Cummings, T.G., & Worley, C.G. (2009). *Organization Development & Change.* Canada: Cengage Learning.

Daftuar, C.N. (1996). HRD Questionnaire. In Sarupria, D.S., Rao T.V. and Sethumadavan P., *Measuring Organizational Climate,* 117-121.

Deckop, J.R., Mangel, R. & Circa, C. (1999). Getting more than you Pay for: Organizational Citizenship and Pay-performance Plans. *Academy of Management Journal,* 42, 420-428.

Delery, J.E., & Doty, D.H. (1996). Modes of Theorizing in Human Resource Management: Tests of Universalistic, Contingency and Configurational Performance Predictions. *Academy of Management Journal,* 39 (4), 802-835.

DeNisi, Angelo S., & Pritchard, Robert D. (2006). Performance Appraisal, Performance Management and Improving Individual Performance: A Motivational Framework. *Management and Organization Review,* 2(2), 253-277.

Dickinson Liz (2009). *An Examination of the Factors Affecting Organizational Citizenship Behavior.* Departmental Honors Thesis, The University of Tennessee at Chattanooga, Tennessee.

Dipboye, R.L., & de Pontbriand, R. (1981). Correlates of Employee Reactions to Performance Appraisals and Appraisal Systems. *Journal of Applied Psychology,* 66 (2), 248-251.

DiPaola, M., & Tschannen-Moran, M. (2001). Organizational Citizenship Behavior in Schools and its Relationships to School Climate. *Journal of School Leadership*, 11 (5), 424-447.

Dobbins, G.H., Cardy, R.L., & Platz-Vieno, S.J. (1990). A Contingency Approach to Appraisal Satisfaction: An Initial Investigation of the Joint Effects of Organizational Variables and Appraisal Characteristics. *Journal of Management,* 16 (3), 619-632.

Dyer, L., & Reeves, T. (1995). Human Resource Strategies and Firm Performance: What do we know and where do we need to go? *International Journal of Human Resource Management*, 6 (3), 656-670.

Eisenberger, R., Huntington, R., Hutchison, S., & Sowa, D.(1986). Perceived Organizational Support. *Journal of Applied Psychology*, 71, 500-507.

Elloy, D. (2012). Effects of Ability Utilization, Job Influence and Organization Commitment on Employee Empowerment: An Empirical Study. *International Journal of Management*, 29 (2), 627-632.

Erdogan, B. (2002). Antecedents and Consequences of Justice Perceptions in Performance Appraisals. *Human Resource Management Review*, 12 (4), 555-578.

Erdogan, B., Kraimer, M.L., & Liden, R.C. (2001). Procedural Justice as a Two Dimensional Construct. *Journal of Applied Behavioral Science*, 37 (2), 205-222.

Facteau, J.D., Dobbins, G.H., Russell, J.E.A., Ladd, R.T., & Kudisch, J.D. (1995). The Influence of General Perceptions of the Training Environment on Pre-training Motivation and Perceived Training Transfer. *Journal of Management*, 21 (1), 1-25.

Facteau, C.L., Facteau, J.D., Schoel, L.C., Russel, J.E.A., & Poteet, M.L. (1998). Reactions of Leaders to 360-degree Feedback from Subordinates and Peers. *Leadership Quarterly*, 9 (4), 427-448.

Farh, J., Earley, P.C., & Lin, S. (1997). Impetus for Action: A Cultural Analysis of Justice and Organizational Citizenship Behavior in Chinese Society. *Administrative Science Quarterly*, 42 (3), 421-444.

Farh, J., Podsakoff, P.M., & Organ, D.W. (1990). Accounting for Organizational Citizenship Behavior: Leader Fairness and Task Scope versus Satisfaction. *Journal of Management*, 16(4), 705-721.

Fatt, C.K., Khin, E.W.S. & Heng, T.N. (2010). The Impact of Organizational Justice on Employee's Job Satisfaction: The Malaysian Companies Perspectives. *American Journal of Economic Business Administration*, 2 (1), 56-63.

Findley, H.M., Mossholder, K.W., & Giles, W.F. (2000). Performance Appraisal Process and System Facets: Relationships with Contextual Performance. *Journal of Applied Psychology*, *85* (4), 634-640.

Fisher, M. (1996). Performance Appraisal Building your Team: The Sunday Times Business Skills Series, *Kogan*, 15-17.

Fisher, G.G., Bulger, C.A. & Smith, C.S. (2009). Beyond Work and Family: A measure of Work/non-work Interference and Enhancement. *Journal of Occupational Health Psychology*, 14(4), 441-456.

Folger, R., & Konovsky, M.A. (1989). Effects of Procedural and Distributive Justice on Reactions to Pay Raise Decisions. *Academy of Management Journal*, 32(1), 115-130.

Ford, D.J. (2000). *Bottom—line Training* (p. 75). New Delhi: Prentice Hall of India Ltd.

Frone, M., & Yardley, J. (1996). Workplace Family-supportive Programmes: Predictors of Employed Parents' Importance Ratings. *Journal of Occupational and Organizational Psychology*, 69 (4), 351-366.

Frone, M., Yardley, J., & Markel, K. (1997). Developing and Testing an Integrative Model of the Work-family Interface. *Journal of Vocational Behaviour*, 50 (2), 145-167.

Fulford, M.D., & Enz, C.A. (1995). The Impact of Empowerment on Service Employees. *Journal of Managerial Issues*, 7(2), 161-75.

Giangreco, Antonio, Sebastiano, Antonio, & Peccei, Riccardo (2009). Trainees' Reactions to Training: An Analysis of the Factors Affecting overall Satisfaction with Training. *The International Journal of Human Resource Management*, 20 (1), 96-111.

Gatewood, R.D., & Rockmore, B.W. (1986). Combining Organizational Manpower and Career Development needs: An Operational Human Resource Planning Model. *Human Resource Planning*, 9 (3), 81-96.

Ghosh, A.K. (2013). Employee Empowerment: A Strategic Tool to Obtain Sustainable Competitive Advantage. *International Journal of Management*, 30 (3), 95-107.

Gilley, J.W., Eggland, S.A., & Gilley, A.M. (2002). *Principles of Human Resource Development*. Cambridge: Perseus Books.

Goldstein, I.L, & Ford, J.K. (2002). *Training in Organizations: Needs Assessment, Development, and Evaluation* (4th ed.). Belmont, CA: Wadswanh.

Greenberg, J. (1993). The Social Side of Fairness: Interpersonal and Informational Classes of Organizational Justice. In R. Cropanzano (Ed.), *Justice in the Workplace: Approaching Fairness in Human Resource Management* (pp. 79-103). Hillsdale, NJ: Erlbaum.

Greenberg, J. (1994). Using Socially Fair Treatment to Promote Acceptance of a Work Site Smoking Ban. *Journal of Applied Psychology*, 79 (2), 288-297.

Greenberg, J. (1987). A Taxonomy of Organizational Justice Theories. *Academy of Management Review*, 12(1), 9-22.

Greenberg, J. (1990). Employee Theft as a Reaction to Underpayment Inequity. The Hidden Cost of Pay Cuts. *Journal of Applied Psychology*, 75 (5), 561-568.

Greenhaus, J.H., & Powell, G.H. (2006). When Work and Family are Allies: A theory of work-family Enrichment. *Academy of Management Review*, 31, 72-92.

Guest, R.H. (1979). Quality of Work Life-learning from Tarrytown. *Harvard Business Review*, 57(4), 76-89.

Guest, D. (1997). Human Resource Management and Performance. *International Journal of Human Resource Management*, 8(3), 263-275.

Guest, D.E. (2002). Perspectives on the Study of Work-life Balance, *Social Science Information*, 41(2), 255-279.

Gultek, M.M., Dodd, T.H., & Guydosh, R.M. (2006). Attitudes towards Wine-service Training and its Influence on Restaurant Wine Sales. *International Journal of Hospitality Management*, 25 (3), 432-436.

Guest, D., & Conway, N. (1998). *Fairness at work and the Psychological Contract*, London: Institute of Personnel and Development.

Hackman, J. R., & Oldham, G. R. (1980) *Work Redesign*, Reading, MA: Addison-Wesley Publishing Company.

Hardy, C., & Leiba-O'Sullivan, S. (1998). The Power behind Empowerment: Implications for Research and Practice. *Human Relations*, 51 (4), 451-483.

Hendry, C. (1991). International Comparisons of Human Resource Management: Putting the Firm in the Frame. *International Journal of Human Resource Management*, 2(3), 415-440.

Houlton III, E. (1998). What is performance? Levels of Performance Revisited. In Torraco R. (Ed.). *The Research Agenda for Improving Performance*. Washington, DC: ISPI Press.

Hughes, J., & Bozioneles, N. (2007). Work-life Balance as Source of Job Dissatisfaction and withdrawal Attitudes-an Exploratory Study on the Views of Male Workers. *Personnel Review*, 36(1), 145-154.

Huselid, M.A. (1995). The Impact of Human Resource Management Practices on turnover, Productivity, and Corporate Financial Performance. *Academy of Management Journal*, 38 (3), 635-672.

Hyman, J., & Summers, J. (2004). Lacking Balance? Work-life Employment Practices in the Modern Economy. *Personnel Review*, 33(4) 418-29.

Hyman, J., Baldry, C., Scholarios, D., & Bunzel, D. (2003), Work-life Imbalance in the New Service Sector Economy. *British Journal of Industrial Relations*, 41 (2), 215-39.

Ilgen, D.R., Fisher, C.D., & Taylor, M.S. (1979). Consequences of Individual Feedback on Behavior in Organizations. *Journal of Applied Psychology*, 64 (4), 349-371.

Jain, Ravindra, & Agrawal, Richa (2007). Indian and International Perspectives on Employee Training Practices: A Trend Report. *South Asian Journal of Management*, 12 (1), 79-100.

Jain, Ravindra, & Kamble, Sachin (2005). An Assessment of Effectiveness of Performance Appraisal System in Selected Large and Medium Size Manufacturing Organizations. *Abhigyan,* 22(4), 28-39.

Jain, Ravindra, & Premkumar (2011). HRD practices in Indian Organizations and their Impact on Productivity of Human Resources. *Management and Labour Studies,* 36(1), 5-30.

Jain, Ravindra, Premkumar, & Kamble, Sachin (2014). HRD system in India: Conceptual Framework, measure Development & Model Fit, *Indian Journal of Industrial Relations,* 49 (2), 230-246.

Jain, V.K., Singhal, K.C., & Singh, V.C. (1997). HRD Climate in Indian Industry. *Productivity,* 37(4), 628-639.

James, L.R., Hater, J.J., Gent, M.J., & Bruni, J.R. (1978). Psychological Climate: Implications from Cognitive Social Learning Theory and Interactional Psychology. *Personnel Psychology,* 31 (4), 783-813.

Jawahar (2006). Correlates of Satisfaction with Performance Appraisal Feedback. *Journal of Labour Research, XXVII* (2), 213-236.

Jennings, P.D., Cyr, D., & Moore, L.F. (1995). Human Resource Management on the Pacific Rim: An Integration. In L.F. Moore & P.D. Jennings (Eds.). *Human Resource Management on the Pacific Rim: Institutions, Practices, and Attitudes* (pp. 351-379). Berlin: de Gruyter.

Joshi, S., Leichne, J., Melanson, K., Pruna, C., Sager, N., Story, C.J., & Williams, K. (2002). Work-life balance: A Case of Social Responsibility or Competitive Advantages? Retrieved from http://www.worklifebalance. com.

Kandula, Srinivas, R. (2001). *Strategic Human Resource Development,* New Delhi, Prentice Hall of India Pvt. Ltd.

Kanter, R.M. (1983). *The Change Masters.* New York: Simon & Schuster.

Kanwar, Y.P.S., Singh, A.K., &, Kodwani, A.D. (2009). Work-life Balance and burnout as Predictors of Job Satisfaction in the IT-ITES Industry. *VISION—The Journal of Business Perspective,* 13(2), 1-12.

Katz, D., & Kahn, R.L. (1966). *The Social Psychology of Organizations.* New York: Wiley.

Keeping, L.M., & Levy, P.E. (2000). Performance Appraisal Reactions: Measurement, Modeling, and method bias. *Journal of Applied Psychology,* 85 (5), 708-23.

Khandwalla, Pradip N (1995). *Management Styles,* New Delhi: Tata McGraw-Hill.

Kilam, I.K., & Kumari, N. (2012). Career Planning & HRD Climate - A Major HR Challenge for Public Sector Banks in India. *Asian Journal of Multidimensional Research, 1* (7), 60-82.

Kim, Namhee (2005). Organizational Interventions Influencing Employee Career Development preferred by different Career Success Orientations. *International Journal of Training and Development*, 9 (1), 47-61.

Kirkpatrick, D.L. (1959). Techniques for Evaluating Training Programs. *Journal of the American Society for Training Directors*, 13(11), 3-9.

Kirkpatrick, D.L. (1994). *Evaluating Training Programs: The Four Levels.* San Francisco: Berretl-Koehler.

Kirkpatrick, D.L., & Kirkpatrick, J.D. (2006). *Evaluating Training Programs: The Four Levels* (3rd ed.). San Francisco, US: Berrett-Koehler.

Koberg, C.S., Boss, R.W., Senjem, J.C., & Goodman, E.A. (1999). Antecedents and Outcomes of Empowerment: Empirical Evidence from the Health Care Industry. *Group and Organization Management*, 24 (1), 71-91.

Konovsky, M.A., & Pugh, S.D. (1994). Citizenship Behavior and Social Exchange. *Academy of Management Journal*, 37 (3), 656-669.

Kossek, E.E., & Ozeki, C. (1998). Work-family Conflict, Policies, and the Job-life Satisfaction Relationship: A Review and Directions for Organizational Behavior-human Resources Research. *Journal of Applied Psychology*, 83 (2), 139-149.

Kossek, E.E., & Ozeki, C. (1999). Bridging the Work-family Policy and Productivity Gap: A Literature Review. *Community, Work & Family*, 2 (1), 7-32.

Kossek, E.E., Colquitt, J.A., & Noe, R.A. (2001). Care-giving decisions, Well-being, and Performance: The Effects of Place and provider as a Function of Dependent Type and Work-family Climates. *Academy of Management Journal*, 44 (1), 29-44.

Kraiger, K, Ford. J.K., & Salas, E. (1993). Application of Cognitive, Skill-based, and Affective theories of Learning Outcomes to New methods of Training Evaluation. *Journal of Applied Psychology*, *78* (2), 311-328.

Kraiger, K., McLinden, D., & Casper, W.J. (2004). Collaborative Planning for Training Impact. *Human Resource Management*, 43(4), 337-351.

Kumar, S. (2005). A Comparative Study of Role Clarity and Work Locus of Control in Banks. *Bombay Psychologist*, 20, 14-19.

Kumar, S., & Patnaik, S.P. (2002). HRD Climate and Attributes of Teachers in JNVS. *International Journal of Training and Development*, *XXXII*(2) 31-37.

Kuvaas, Bard (2006). Performance Appraisal Satisfaction and Employee Outcomes: Mediating and Moderating Roles of Work Motivation. *International Journal of Human Resource Management*, 17(3), 504-522.

Lambert, S.J. (2000). Added Benefits: The Link between Work-life Benefits and Organizational Citizenship Behavior. *Academy of Management Journal*, 43 (5), 801-815.

Lambert, S.J. (2006). Both Art and Science: Employing Organizational Documentation in Workplace-based Research. In Pitt-Catsouphes, M., Kossek, E.E., & Sweet, S. (Eds.). *The Work and Family Handbook: Multi-disciplinary Perspectives, methods, and Approaches*. (pp. 503-525). Mahwah, New Jersey: Lawrence Erlbaum Associates.

Latting, J.K. (1992). Giving Corrective Feedback: A Decisional Analysis. *Social Work*, 37(5), 424-431.

Lawler, E.E. (1986). *High-Involvement Management*. San Francisco: Jossey-Bass.

Lawler III, E.E. (2003). Reward Practices and Performance Management System Effectiveness. *Organizational Dynamics*, 32 (4), 396-404.

Lee, C.H., & Bruvold, N.T. (2003). Creating value for Employees: Investment in Employee Development. *The International Journal of Human Resource Management*, 14(6), 981-1000.

LePine, J.A., Erez, A., & Johnson, D.E. (2002). The Nature and Dimensionality of Organizational Citizenship Behavior: A Critical Review and Meta-analysis. *Journal of Applied Psychology*, 87(1), 52-65.

Leventhal, G.S. (1976). The Distribution of Rewards and Resources in Groups and Organizations. In L. Berkowitz & W. Walster (Eds.), *Advances in Experimental Social Psychology*, Vol. 9 (pp. 91-131). New York: Academic Press.

Leventhal, G.S. (1980). What should be done with Equity Theory? New Approaches to the Study of Fairness in Social Relationships. In K. Gergen, M. Greenberg, & R. Willis (Eds.), *Social exchange: Advances in Theory and Research* (pp. 27-55). New York: Plenum Press.

Levy, P.E., & Williams, J.R. (2004). The Social Context of Performance Appraisal: A Review and Framework for the Future. *Journal of Management*, 30 (6), 881-905.

Liddicoat, L. (2003). Stakeholders Perceptions of Family-friendly Workplaces: An Examination of Six New Zealand Organizations, *Asian Pacific Journal of Human Resources*, 41(3), 354-370.

Liden, R.C., & S. Arad (1996). A Power Perspective of Empowerment and Work Groups: Implications for Human Resources Management Research. (pp. 205-251). In G.R. Ferris (Ed.). *Research in Personnel and Human Resources Management*, 14, Greenwich, CT: JAI Press.

MacKenzie, S.B., Podsakoff, P.M., & Fetter, R. (1993). The Impact of Organizational Citizenship Behavior on Evaluations of Sales Performance. *Journal of Marketing*, 57, 70-80.

McDonald, K.S., Hite, L.M., & Gilbreath, B. (2002). Non-salaried US Employees' Careers: An Exploratory Study. *Career Development International*, 7 (7), 398-406.

Mc Donald, K.S., & Hite, L.M. (2005). Reviving the Relevance of Career Development in Human Resource Development. *Human Resource Development Review*, 4 (4), 418-439.

McLean, G.N., & McLean, L. (2001). If we can't define HRD in One Country, how can we define it in an International Context?. *Human Resource Development International*, 4 (3), 313-326.

Maume, D.J., & Houston, P. (2001). Job Segregation and Gender Differences in Work–family Spillover among White–collar Workers. *Journal of Family and Economic Issues*, 22 (2), 171-189.

Menon, S.T. (2001). Employee Empowerment: An Integrative Psychological Approach. *Applied Psychology: An International Review*, 50(1), 153-180.

Miller, L.P. (2002). *Perception of Training and Non-training Managers of Organizational Impact measure based on Design Intent*. Doctoral Dissertation, North Carolina State University, North Carolina, USA.

Mishra, P., & Bhardwaj, G. (2002). HRD Climate: An Empirical Study Among Private Sector Managers. *Indian Journal of Industrial Relations*, 38(1), 66-80.

Mittal, Shweta (2013). HRD Climate in Public & Private Sector Banks. *The Indian Journal of Industrial Relations*, 49 (1), 123-141.

Moideenkutty, U. (2000). Equity Sensitivity, Organizational Justice, and Organizational Citizenship Behaviour: A Relational Study. *Management and Change*, 6(2), 279-294.

Monis, H., & Sreedhara, T.N. (2010). Correlates of Employee Satisfaction with Performance Appraisal System in Foreign MNC BPOs Operating in India. *Annals of the University of Petrosani, Economics*, 10(4), 215-224.

Moorman, R.H. (1991). Relationship between Organizational Justice and Organizational Citizenship Behaviors: do Fairness Perceptions Influence Employee Citizenship? *Journal of Applied Psychology*, 76(6), 845-855.

Moorman, R.H. (1993). The Influence of Cognitive and Affective based Job Satisfaction measures on the Relationship between Satisfaction and Organizational Citizenship Behavior. *Human Relations*, 46 (6), 756-776.

Moorman, R.H., & Blakely, G.L. (1995). Individualism-Collectivism as an Individual difference Predictor of Organizational Citizenship Behavior. *Journal of Organizational Behavior*, 16 (2), 127-142.

Moorman, R.H., Blakely, G.L., & Niehoff, B.P. (1998). Does perceived Organizational Support Mediate the Relationship between Procedural Justice and Organizational Citizenship Behavior? *Academy of Management Journal*, 41 (3), 351-357.

Moorman, R.H., Niehoff, B.P., Organ, D.W. (1993). Treating Employees Fairly and Organizational Citizenship Behavior: Sorting the Effects of Job Satisfaction, Organizational Commitment, and Procedural Justice. *Employee Responsibilities and Rights Journal*, 6 (3), 209-225.

Morrison, E.W. (1996). Organizational Citizenship Behaviour as a Critical Link between HR Practices and Service Quality. *Human Resource Management*, 35 (4), 493-512.

Murphy, K.R., & Cleveland, J.N. (1991). *Performance Appraisal: An Organizational Perspective*. Boston: Allyn and Bacon.

Nadiri, H. & Tanova, C. (2010). An Investigation of the Role of Justice in turnover Intentions, Job Satisfaction, and Organizational Citizenship Behavior in Hospitality Industry. *International Journal of Hospitality Management*, 29 (1), 33-41.

Nadler, L. (1969). The Variety of Training Roles. *Industrial & Commercial Training*, 1(1), 33-37.

Newman, A., Thanacoody, R., & Hui, W. (2011). The Impact of Employee Perceptions of Training on Organizational Commitment and Turnover Intentions: A Study of Multinationals in the Chinese Service Sector. *The International Journal of Human Resource Management*, 22 (8), 1765-1787.

Niehoff, B.P., Moorman, R.H. (1993). Justice as a Mediator of the Relationship between methods of Monitoring and Organizational Citizenship Behavior. *Academy of Management Journal*, 36 (3), 527-556.

Nishii, L.H., & Wright, P. (2008). Variability at Multiple Levels of Analysis: Implications for Strategic Human Resource Management. In D.B. Smith (Ed.). The People make the Place. Mahwah, NJ: Lawrence Erlbaum Associates.

Noe, R.A., & Wilk, S.L. (1993). Investigation of the Factors that Influence Employees' Participation in Development Activities. *Journal of Applied. Psychology*, 78 (2), 291-302.

Nonaka, I. (1988). Toward Middle-up-down Management: Accelerating Information Creation. *Sloan Management Review*, 29(3), 9-18.

Noorliza, K., & Hasni, M. (2006). The Effects of Total Quality Management Practices on Employees Work related Attitudes. *The TQM Magazine*, 18 (1), 30-33.

Norris-Watts, C., & Levy, P.E. (2004). The Mediating Role of Affective Commitment in the Relation of the Feedback Environment to Work Outcomes. *Journal of Vocational Behavior*, 65(3), 351-365.

O'Bannon, D. P., &. Pearce, C.L. (1999). A Quasi-experiment of Gain-sharing in Service Organization: Implications of Organizational Citizenship Behavior and Pay Satisfaction. *Journal of Management Issues, 11*, 363-378.

Oostrom, J.K., & van Mierlo, H. (2008). An Evaluation of an Aggression Management Training Program to Cope with Workplace Violence in the Healthcare Sector. *Research in Nursing & Health*, 31 (4), 320-328.

Organ, D.W. (1988). *Organizational Citizenship Behavior: The Good Soldier Syndrome*. Lexington, MA: Lexington Books.

Organ, D.W. (1997). Organizational Citizenship Behavior: It's Construct Clean-up Time. *Human Performance*, 10 (2), 85-97.

Organ, D.W., Moorman, R.H. (1993). Fairness and Organizational Citizenship Behavior: what are the Connections? *Social Justice Research*, 6(1), 5-18.

Pace, R.W. (2002). *Organisation Dynamism*. West Port, CT: Quorum.

Pajo, K., Coetzer, A., & Guenole, N. (2010), Formal Development Opportunities and withdrawal Behaviors by Employees in Small and Medium-sized Enterprises. *Journal of Small Business Management*, 48 (3), 281-301.

Paine, J.B., & Organ, D.W. (2000). The Cultural Matrix of Organizational Citizenship Behavior: Some Preliminary Conceptual and Empirical Observations. *Human Resource Management Review*, 10 (1), 45-59.

Pardo del Val, Manuela, & Lloyd, Bruce (2003). Measuring Empowerment. *Leadership and Organization Development Journal*, 24(2), 102-108.

Pareek, U, & Rao, T.V. (1975). HRD System in Larsen & Toubro, Unpublished Consultancy Report. Indian Institute of Management, Ahmedabad, Ahmedabad.

Parker, L.E., & Price, L.H. (1994). Empowered Managers and Empowered Workers: The Effects Managerial Support and Managerial Perceived Control on Workers' Sense of Control Over Decision making. *Human Relations*, 47(8), 911-928.

Parasuraman, S., Purohit, Y, Godshalk, V., & Beutell, N. (1996). Work and Family Variables, Entrepreneurial Career Success, and Psychological well-being. *Journal of Vocational Behaviour*, 48 (3), 275-300.

Pattanayak, Biswajit (2000). Effects of Shift Work and Hierarchical Position on Satisfaction, Commitment, Stress and HRD Climate: A Study on an Integrated Steel Plant. *Management & Labour Studies*, 25(2), 126-135.

Patel, M.K. (2005). *Case Studies on HRD Practices*. New Delhi: Anmol Publications Pvt. Ltd.

Pearson C.A.L., & Duffy C. (1999). The Importance of the Job Content and Social Information on Organizational Commitment and Job Satisfaction: A Study in Australian and Malaysian Nursing Contexts. *Asia Pacific Journal of Human Resources,* 36(3), 17-30.

Peccei, R., & Rosenthal, P. (2001). Delivering Customer-oriented Behavior through Empowerment: An Empirical Test of HRM Assumptions. *Journal of Management Studies,* 38(6), 831-857.

Pethe, S. Chaudhary, S. & Dhar, U. (1999). *Occupational Self– Efficacy Scale and Manual.* National Psychological Corporation, Agra.

Pfeffer, J. (1998). Seven Practices of Successful Organizations. *California Management Review,* 40(2), 96-124.

Pfeffer, J., & Veiga, F. (1999). Putting People First for Organizational Success. *Academy of Management Executive,* 13(2), 37-48.

Podsakoff, P.M., Ahearne M., & MacKenzie S.B. (1997). Organizational Citizenship Behavior and the Quantity and Quality for Work Group Performance. *Journal of Applied Psychology,* 82 (2), 262-270.

Podsakoff, P.M., & MacKenzie, S.B. (1994). Organizational Citizenship Behavior and Sales unit Effectiveness. *Journal of Marketing Research,* 31 (3), 351-363.

Podsakoff, P.M., & MacKenzie, S.B. (1994). An Examination of the Psychometric Properties and Nomological Validity of some Revised and Reduced Substitutes for Leadership Scales. *Journal of Applied Psychology,* 79 (5), 702-713.

Podsakoff, P.M., MacKenzie, S.B., Paine, J.B., & Bachrach, D.G. (2000). Organizational Citizenship Behaviors: A Critical Review of the Theoretical and Empirical Literature and Suggestions for Future Research. *Journal of Management,* 26 (3), 513-563.

Priyadarshini, R., & Venkatapathy, R. (2003). Impact of HRD on Organizational Effectiveness in the Banking Industry. *Prajnan,* 32(2), 125-147.

Prokopenko, J. (1987). *Productivity Management: A Practical Handbook.* Geneva: International Labor Organization.

Psoinos, A., & Smithson, S. (2002). Employee Empowerment in Manufacturing: A Study of Organizations in the UK. *New Technology, Work and Employment,* 17(2), 132-48.

Purang, P. (2006). HRD Climate: A Comparative Analysis of Public, Private and Multinational Organizations. *Indian Journal of Industrial Relations,* 41(3), 407-419.

Purang, P. (2008). Dimensions of HRD Climate Enhancing Organizational Commitment in Indian Organizations. *Indian Journal of Industrial Relations*, 43 (4), 528-546.

Purcell, J. (1999). Best Practice and Best Fit: Chimera or cul-de-sac?. *Human Resource Management Journal*, 9(3), 26-41.

Rajeev, P., Madan, M.S., & Jayarajan, K. (2009). Revisiting Kirkpatrick's model – An Evaluation of an Academic Training Course. *Current Science*, 96(2), 272-276.

Randolph, W.A. (2000). Re-thinking Empowerment: Why is it so hard to achieve? *Organizational Dynamics*, 29 (2), 94-107.

Rao, P.S. (2008). *Essentials of Human Resource Management and Industrial Relations* (3rd Revised Edition). Mumbai: Himalaya Publishing House.

Rao, T.V. (1986). Integrated Human Resource Development Systems. In Rao, T.V., & Pereira, D.F. (Eds.), *Recent Experiences in Human Resource Development* (p. 5). New Delhi: Oxford & IBH.

Rao, T.V., & E. Abraham (1986). Human Resource Development Climate in Indian Organization. In Rao, T.V., & Pereira, D.F. (Eds.), *Recent Experiences in Human Resource Development* (pp. 70-98). Oxford & IBH: New Delhi.

Rao, T.V (1987). Planning for Human Resources Development. *Vikalpa*, 12(3), 46-51.

Rao, T.V., & Abraham, E. (1990). The HRD Climate Survey. In J.W. Pfeiffer (Ed.). *The 1990 Annual Developing Human Resources*. San Diego, CA: University Associates.

Rao, T.V. (1992). HRD in Voltas. In Pareek, U., & Rao, T.V. (Eds.), *Designing and Managing Human Resource Systems* (pp. 352-354). New Delhi: Oxford & IBH.

Rao, T.V., E. Abraham, & Baburaj V., Nair (Eds.). (1993). HRD Philosophies and Concepts: The Indian Perspective. Ahmedabad: National HRD Network.

Rao T.V., Rao, Raju, & Yadav, Taru (2007). A Study of HRD Concepts, Structure of HRD Departments, and HRD Practices in India. *Vikalpa*, 26(1), 49-63.

Raub, S., & Robert, C. (2007). *Empowerment and Organizational Citizenship: Moderation by Culture in a Multi-national Sample*. In Academy of Management Proceedings (Vol. 2007, No. 1, pp. 1-6). Academy of Management.

Raub, S., & Robert, C. (2013). Empowerment, Organizational Commitment, and Voice Behavior in the Hospitality Industry Evidence from a Multinational Sample. *Cornell Hospitality Quarterly*, 54(2), 136-148.

Rego, A., & Cunha, M.P.E. (2008). Organizational Citizenship Behaviours and Effectiveness: An Empirical Study in Two Small Insurance Companies. *The Service Industries Journal*, 28 (4), 541-554.

Rodrigues, L.L.R., & Chincholkar, A.M. (2005). Benchmarking the HR Practices of an Engineering Institute with Public Sector Industry for Performance Enhancement. *International Journal of Training and Development*, 9(1), 6-20.

Russell, S., Terborg, I.R., & Powers, M. L. (1985). Organizational Performances and Organizational Level Training and Support. *Personnel Psychology*, 38, 849-863.

Sahoo, C.K., Behera, & Tripathy, S.K. (2010). Employee Empowerment and Individual Commitment. An Analysis from Integrative Review of Research. *Employment Relations Record*, 10(1), 40-56.

Saklani, D.R. (2004). Quality of Work Life in the Indian Context: An Empirical Investigation. *Decision*, 31 (2), 101-135.

Saraswathi, S. (2010). Human Resources Development Climate: An Empirical Study. *International Journal of Innovation, Management and Technology*, 1(2), 174-179.

Saxena, P.K. (2011). Measuring the Effectiveness of Training Programmes: A Study with Respect to State Bank of Indore. Unpublished Thesis, Devi Ahilya University, Indore, MP.

Saxena, K., & Tiwari, P. (2009, October 16-17). HRD Climate in Selected Public Sector Banks: An Empirical Study. Paper Presented at the *9th Global Conference on Business and Economics, UK.*

Schappe, S. (1998). The Influence of Job Satisfaction, Organizational Commitment and Fairness Perceptions on Organizational Citizenship Behavior. *Journal of Applied Psychology*, 132 (3), 277-290.

Schaufeli, W.B., Salanova, M., Gonzalez-Roma, V., & Bakker, A.B. (2002). The measurement of Engagement and burnout: A Two-sample Confirmatory Factor Analytic Approach. *Journal of Happiness Studies*, 3(1), 71-92.

Schneider, B., & Reichers, A.E. (1983). On the Etymology of Climates. *Personnel Psychology*, 36, 19-39.

Scott-Ladd, B., & C.C.A. Chan (2004). Emotional Intelligence and Participation in Decision-making: Strategies for Promoting Organizational Learning and Change. *Strategic Change*, 13 (2), 95-105.

Scott, D. (1980). The Causal Relationship between Trust and the Assessed Value of Management by Objectives. *Journal of Management*, 6(2), 157-175.

Seibert, S.E., Silver, S.R., & Randolph, W.A. (2004). Taking Empowerment to the Next Level: A Multiple-level Model of Empowerment, Performance, and Satisfaction. *Academy of Management Journal,* 47(3), 332-49.

Settoon, R.P., & Mossholder, K.W. (2002). Relationship Quality and Relationship context as Antecedents of Person- and Task-focused Interpersonal Citizenship Behavior. *Journal of Applied Psychology,* 87(2), 255-267.

Shrivastava, A., & Purang, P. (2011). Employee Perceptions of Performance Appraisals: A Comparative Study on Indian Banks. *International Journal of Human Resource Management,* 22(3), 632-647.

Shrivastava, A., & Purang, P. (2012). Effect of Age on Fairness Perceptions: A Study of Two Indian Banks, *Indian Journal of Industrial Relations,* 48(1), 150-159.

Sitzmann, T., Brown, K.G., Casper, W., Ely, K., & Zimmerman, R.D. (2008). A Review and Meta-analysis of the Nomological Network of Trainee Reactions. *Journal of Applied Psychology,* 93 (2), 280-95.

Sheppard, B.H., R.J. Lewicki, & J.W. Minton (1992). *Organizational Justice: The Search for Fairness in the Workplace.* Lexington, MA: Lexington Books.

Simons, T., & Roberson, Q. (2003). Why Managers should Care about Fairness: The Effects of Aggregate Justice Perceptions on Organizational Outcomes. *Journal of Applied Psychology,* 88(3), 432-443.

Simonsen, P. (1997). *Promoting a Development Culture in your Organization.* Palo Alto, CA: Davies-Black.

Singh, S.K. (1998). Human Resource Development Climate: Interventions and Challenges. *Indian Journal of Training and Development,* 28(3), 23-27.

Skarlicki, D.P., & Folger, R. (1997). Retaliation in the Workplace: The Role of Distributive, Procedural, and Interactional Justice. *Journal of Applied Psychology,* 82 (3), 434-443.

Skarlicki, D.P., & Latham, G.P. (1995). Organizational Citizenship Behavior and Performance in a University Setting. *Canadian Journal of Administrative Sciences,* 12 (3), 175-181.

Skarlicki, D.P., & Latham, G.P. (1997). Leadership Training in Organizational Justice to Increase Citizenship Behavior within a Labor Union: A Replication. *Personnel Psychology,* 50(3), 617-633.

Smith, C.A., Organ, D., & Near, J. (1983). Organizational Citizenship Behavior: Its Nature and Antecedents. *Journal of Applied Psychology,* 68(4), 653-663.

Solkhe, Ajay, & Chaudhary, Nirmala (2011). HRD Climate and Job Satisfaction: An Empirical Investigation. *International Journal of Computing and Business Research*, 2(2), 1-20.

Sparrow, P.R., & Budhwar, P. (1997). Competition and Change: Mapping the Indian HRM Recipe against the World Wide Patterns. *Journal of World Business*, 32 (3), 224-242.

Spreitzer, G. (1995). Psychological Empowerment in the Workplace: Dimensions, measurement, and Validation. *Academy of Management Journal*, 38(5), 1442-1465.

Spreitzer, G.M., Kizilos, M.A., & Nason, S.W. (1997). A Dimensional Analysis of the Relationship between Psychological Empowerment and Effectiveness, Satisfaction, and Strain. *Journal of Management*, 23(5), 679-704.

Srimannarayana, M. (2007). Human Resource Development Climate in a Dubai Organization. *Indian Journal of Industrial Relations*, 43(1), 1-12.

Srimannarayana, M. (2008). Human Resource Development Climate in India, *Indian Journal of Industrial Relations*, 44 (2), 248-255.

Sturges, J., & Guest, D. (2004). Working to Live or Living to Work? Work/life Balance Early in the Career. *Human Resource Management Journal*, 14(4), 5-20.

Sun, L.Y., Aryee, S., & Law, K.S. (2007). High-performance Human Resource Practices, Citizenship Behavior, and Organizational Performance: A Relational Perspective. *Academy of Management Journal*, 50(3), 558-577.

Sugrue, B., & Rivera, R.J. (2005). State of the Industry: ASDT's Annual Review of U.S. and International Trends in Workplace Learning and Performance. Alexandria, VA: ASDT.

Swanson, R.A., & Holton, III, E. F. (2001) *Foundations of Human Resource Development*. San Francisco: Berrett-Koehler Publishers Inc.

Swanson, R.A., & Holton III, E.F. (2009) *Foundations of Human Resource Development*, 2nd Edition. San Francisco: Berret & Koehler Publishers.

Taylor, M.S., Masterson, S.S., Renard, M.K., & Tracy, K.B. (1998). Managers' Reactions to Procedurally just Performance Management Systems. *Academy of Management Journal*, 41(5), 568-579.

Thibaut, & Walker, L. (1975). *Procedural Justice: A Psychological Analysis*. Hillsdale, NJ: Erlbaum.

Thomas, K.W., & Velthouse, B.A. (1990). Cognitive Elements of Empowerment: An "Interpretative" Model of Intrinsic Task Motivation. *Academy of Management Review*, 15(4), 666-681.

Thurston, P.W. Jr. (2001). *Clarifying the Structure of Justice using Fairness Perceptions of Performance Appraisal Practice*. Unpublished Doctoral Dissertation, Albany, NY.

Tian, J., Atkinson, N.L., Portnoy, B., & Gold, R.S. (2007). A Systematic Review of Evaluation in Formal Continuing Medical Education. *Journal of Continuing Education in the Health Professions,* 27(1), 16-27.

Totawar, A., & Nambudiri, R. (2011). *Organizational Justice, Job Satisfaction and the Mediating Role of Quality of Work Life.* Contemporary Research Issues and Challenges in Emerging Economies (pp. 160178). eProceedings for 2011 International Research Conference and Colloquium.

Todd, S.Y. (2003). *A Causal Model Depicting the Influence of Selected Task and Employee Variables on Organizational Citizenship Behavior.* Ph.D. Dissertation, Florida State University.

Tremblay, M., Rondeau, A., & Lemelin, M. (1998). Do Innovative HR Practices Influence Blue-collar Workers' Mobilization?. In GRH Face à une crise: GRH en crise? (pp. 97-109). Montréal, Canada: Presses HEC

Truss, C., Gratton, L., Hope-Hailey, V., McGovern, P., & Stiles, P. (1997). Soft and Hard Models of Human Resource Management: A Reappraisal. *Journal of Management Studies,* 34(1), 53-73.

Turnipseed, D.L., & Rassuli, A. (2005). Performance Perceptions of Organizational Citizenship Behaviors at Work: A Bi-level Study among Managers and Employees. *British Journal of Management,* 16 (3), 231-244.

Tyler, T.R., & Bies, R.J. (1990). Beyond Formal Procedures: The Interpersonal Context of Procedural Justice. In J. Carroll (Ed.), *Applied Social Psychology and Organizational Settings* (pp. 77-98). Hillsdale, NJ: Erlbaum.

Tyler, T.R. (1988). What is Procedural Justice-criteria used by Citizens to Assess the Fairness of Legal Procedures. *Law and Society Review,* 22, 301-335.

van Dijk, M.S. (2004). Career Development within HRD: Foundation or Fad? Proceedings of the Academy of Human Resource Development Conference (pp. 771-778). USA.

Van Dyne, L., Graham, J.G., & Dienesch, R.M. (1994). Organizational Citizenship Behavior: Construct Redefinition, Operationalization, and Validation. *Academy of Management Journal,* 37, 765-802.

Van Dyne, L., LePine, J.A. (1998). Helping and Voice Extra-role Behaviors: Evidence of Construct and Predictive Validity. *Academy of Management Journal,* 41 (1), 108-119.

Van Scotter, J.R., & Motowidlo, S.J. (1996). Interpersonal Facilitation and Job Dedication as Separate Facets of Contextual Performance. *Journal of Applied Psychology,* 81(5), 525-531.

van Steenbergen, E.F., & Ellemers, N. (2009). Is Managing the Work–family Interface Worthwhile? Benefits for Employee Health and Performance. *Journal of Organizational Behaviour,* 30 (5), 617-642.

Vandenberg, R.J., Richarson, H.A., & Eastman, L.J. (1999). The Impact of High-involvement Work Process on Organizational Effectiveness. *Group & Organization Management*, 24 (3), 300-339.

Vanyperen, N.W., van den Berg, A.E., & Willering, M. (1999). Towards a Better Understanding of the Link between Participation in Decision-making and Organizational Citizenship Behaviour: A Multilevel Analysis. *Journal of Occupational and Organizational Psychology*, 72 (3), 377-392.

Vasugi, S.P.M., Kaviatha, F.S., & Prema, R. (2011). An Empirical Investigation on Employee Empowerment Practices in Indian Software Industries. *Interdisciplinary Journal of Contemporary Research in Business*, 2(11), 668-674.

Vigoda-Gadot, E. (2007). Redrawing the Boundaries of OCB? An Empirical Examination of Compulsory Extra-role Behaviour in the Workplace. *Journal of Business and Psychology*, *21* (3), 377-405.

Walton, R.E. (1975). Criteria for Quality of Working Life. In Davis, L.E., Cherns, A.B. & Associates (Eds.). *The Quality of Working Life* (pp. 91-104). New York, NY: The Free Press.

Warr, P., Allan, C., & Birdi, K. (1992). Predicting three Levels of Training Outcome. *Journal of Occupational and Organizational Psychology*, 72(3), 352-372.

Warr, P., & Bunce, D. (1995). Trainee Characteristics and the Outcomes of Open Learning. *Personnel Psychology*, 48 (2), 347-374.

Wei, Y.C., Han, T.S., & Hsu, I.C. (2010). High-performance HR Practices and OCB: A Cross-level Investigation of a Causal Path. *The International Journal of Human Resource Management*, 21(10), 1631-1648.

Werner J.M., & DeSimone, R.L. (2006). *Human Resource Development*. (4th ed.) Mason, Ohio: Thomson-Southwestern.

White, M., Hill S., McGovern, P.Mills, C., & Smeaton, D. (2003). 'High-performance' Management Practices, Working Hours and Work-life Balance. *British Journal of Industrial Relations*, 41(2), 175-195.

Williams, L.J., & Anderson, S.E. (1991). Job Satisfaction and Organization Commitment as Predictors or Organizational Citizenship and in-role Behaviors. *Journal of Management*, 17(3), 601-617.

Wils, T., Guerin, G., & Bernard, R. (1993). Career System as a Configuration of Career Management Activities. *The International Journal of Career Management*, 5(2), 11-15.

Wilkinson, A. (1998). Empowerment: Theory and Practice, *Personnel Review*, 27 (1), 40-56.

Wilson, S., & Coolican, M.J. (1996). How High and Low Self-empowered Teachers Work with Colleagues and School Principals. *The Journal of Educational Thought*, 30 (2), 99-118.

Wright, T.A., & Cropanzano, R. (2004). The Role of Psychological well-being in Job Performance: A Fresh Look at an Age-old Quest. *Organizational Dynamics*, 33, 338-351.

Yoon, M.H., & Suh, J. (2003). Organizational Citizenship Behaviors and Service Quality as External Effectiveness of Contact Employees. *Journal of Business Research*, 56 (8), 597-611.

Zheng, W., Zhang, M., & Li, H. (2012). Performance Appraisal Process and Organizational Citizenship Behavior. *Journal of Managerial Psychology*, 27(7), 732-752.

Index

❒ ❒ ❒ ❒ ❒